RABBI
MOSHE CHAIM LUZZATTO

RABBI
MOSHE CHAIM LUZZATTO

HIS LIFE AND WORKS

YIRMEYAHU BINDMAN

JASON ARONSON INC.
Northvale, New Jersey
London

For credits, see page 177.

This book was set in 12 pt. Antiqua by Alpha Graphics, Pittsfield, New Hampshire, and printed by Haddon Craftsmen in Scranton, Pennsylvania.

Library of Congress Cataloging-in-Publication Data

Bindman, Yirmeyahu
    Rabbi Moshe Chaim Luzzatto : his life and works / Yirmeyahu Bindman.
        p. cm.
    Includes index.
    "The works of Ramchal : a bibliography" : p.
    ISBN 1-56821-293-3
    1. Luzzatto, Moshe Hayyim, 1707–1747. 2. Rabbis—Biography.
  3. Authors, Hebrew—18th century—Biography. 4. Judaism.
I. Title.
BM755.L78B56   1995
892.4'13—dc20
[B]   94-12660

Manufactured in the United States of America. Jason Aronson Inc. offers books and cassettes. For information and catalog write to Jason Aronson Inc., 230 Livingston Street, Northvale, New Jersey 07647.

CONTENTS

PREFACE AND ACKNOWLEDGMENTS

Most of the Ramchal's remaining manuscripts are in the library of the Jewish Theological Seminary, although there are examples in the Jewish National and University Library in Jerusalem, and a few also remain in private hands. They were investigated, cataloged, and printed by the American researcher Dr. Simon Ginzburg during the early years of this century, and his bibliography is still standard.

The Ramchal's major trilogy of expositional works (*The Way of God, The Knowing Heart*, and *The Path of the Just*) has been translated into English and is available in parallel text from Feldheim Publishers, POB 6525, Jerusalem, or 200 Airport Executive Park, Spring Valley, NY 10977, separately or as a set. Translations from these works, by R. Shraga Silberstein and R. Aryeh Kaplan, *zt"l*, have been used by permission. All other verse and prose translations are by the author.

I would like to thank my teachers, R. Shneur Zalman Gafni, R. Yitzchak Ginsburgh, and R. Chaim Lipshitz, without whose help this book could not have been written, and who have guided so many people into the paths of truth.

References to Feldheim translations are to their page numbers and to letters are from *Yarim Moshe*, Mate Yosef edition, 1982. References to prayers are from Shalom Ullman edition, 1979, references to *maamarim* are from Lewin-Epstein edition, 1972, and references to poems are from Gutenberg edition.

Collections of the Ramchal's works published since this book was compiled are by Mossad ha-Rav Kook, Jerusalem.

1

Jewish Padua
and Its Time

The year was 1707; the kingdoms of England and
Scotland had recently signed themselves into
union; the colony of Georgia, last of the thirteen,
was about to be founded. France was approaching
the end of the reign of Louis XIV, the "Sun King,"
most brilliant monarch of the globe, the would-be
unifier of Europe under whose benevolent despo-
tism the country had reached an unprecedented
unity and plenitude. And Italy? Italy was in slum-
ber. Exhausted by internecine warfare, reconciled
to the rule of the pope over its fairest provinces, it
rested on its heroic past, prosperous and settled
enough to rebuild and enjoy its cultural supremacy in the French shadow while still remaining
attached to the archaic political organization that
was its heritage from remotest antiquity.

The Jews prospered along with the country;
few in number except in Rome, they had retained

their foothold in the greatest cities since the tur-
bulent times of the Renaissance, when successive
local expulsions had been the rule. During that
time, the great Rabbi Ovadia Sforno had taught for
a generation at Bologna and the Kabbalah source-
book *Tree of Life* had come from the hand of Rabbi
Chaim Vital. Throughout their residence Italian
Jews had rarely been without a leader of this stature, and it was said that this small community had
produced more first-rank scholars for its size than
any other in the Jewish world. This time was to be
no exception; for it was in the year 1707 that a son
was born in Padua to Rabbi Yaakov Chai Luzzatto
and his wife, Diamante: Moshe Chaim, future
author of some of the most lucid expositions ever
to come from a Jewish pen, whose embattled life
was to end in the peace of the Holy Land.

Nearly three hundred years before, the remote
ancestors of the family had come to Italy from the
village of Lausitz in Bavaria. They settled first in
Venice, then at the peak of its power and influence,
a trading capital that attracted Jews from all over
the world. In the Italy of the Renaissance almost
all the different rites of the Jewish dispersion were
in use side by side; each group formed its own
community and lived as its ancestors had done.
There were Sephardi refugees in the seaports, in-
vited there by ambitious rulers, and Ashkenazim
in the cities of the north. Rome had its large Italyeni
community, the descendants of Jews brought as
prisoners after the capture of Judea, who recited
the *Kol Nidrei* in Hebrew instead of Aramaic as an
indication of their ties with the Land of Israel.

Under papal rule the lot of the Jews was harsh; kept as a symbol of ideological victory, they were subjected to exactions and felt trapped in a swamp of backwardness and economic decline. But in Venice it was different.

CITY OF THE SEA

The city that grew into the mighty republic had an amazing history. Growing from a cluster of inhabitants who sought safety from marauders on the islands of the lagoon, it became a vast commercial power, prospering on the trade between Europe and the East. Its elected leader, the doge, held office for life, and it acquired a reputation as a dynamic, forward-looking state where the best minds in every form of enterprise could find scope for their talents. The Jewish community was composed of five major groupings known as "nations," and the city coined the word *ghetto* for their residential quarter. Shakespeare's picture of brash good humor typified the image that spread to every corner of Europe with money to spend on luxury. All eyes were turned to Venice; the doge was one of the world's most powerful politicians, and amid pomp and glitter he would symbolize his state's dependence on the sea in an annual ceremony of "marriage," in which a gold ring was tossed into the waters. He was master of an empire in the East whose naval battles with the Turks culminated in the mighty clash of Lepanto, the last encounter between fleets propelled by oars.

Whole provinces of the Italian mainland came under the republic's sway. But the centuries passed; the nations of Western Europe explored for sea routes to India and found America in the process. The Levantine trade went elsewhere; the Turks began to move into Europe in strength, and after the last effective doge gambled all the state's reserves on a disastrous war for imperial stature, the downfall of Venice was sealed. It remained a prosperous manufacturing town, but its long twilight as a home of diversion for the Continent's privileged classes lasted until the terse decree of Napoleon—"the Venetian Republic no longer exists"—struck it from the register of history.

At the start of the eighteenth century, however, it was still a city in its own right, producing glassware and woolen goods for export. Somewhat earlier one of its travelers in the East had discovered the drinking of coffee and begun importing the beans into Europe. The Western world's first coffeehouse was established in the Piazza San Marco, beginning the tradition of wit and sociability that stemmed from this delightful relief. The Jewish community was still substantial, and the Luzzatto family had struck deep roots within it, giving their name to one of the synagogues.

When the city of Padua on the mainland was annexed in 1405, a branch of the family moved there. Padua was also a wealthy town, but the Venetians valued it chiefly for its famous university, as their city did not have one of its own. Founded early in medieval times, the university was subsidized heavily by the Venetian government after the takeover, soon gaining a position of world renown. There was a scientific faculty, which had had Galileo as professor, and one of the oldest and finest medical schools in the world, almost unique in extending its degree to Jewish candidates. These came to study from far away, even from Germany and Poland, usually rising to positions of eminence on returning home. Some of the keenest and most sincere intellects in the Jewish world were thus gathered in Padua, thriving in the high standards of talmudic learning established there in early times.

There was a special atmosphere in the city, one of very few major intellectual centers for both Jews and gentiles in their different ways. Here in 1344 Jacopo de' Dondi had invented the clock dial, and his son Giovanni had completed an amazing timepiece-planetarium, so complicated and exact that people came from abroad to see it and to meet its constructor. This spirit showed in the openness and regularity of the architecture, set in the sunny, humid valley of the Po. Cesare Faligno writes in his *Story of Padua* (London: J. M. Dent & Sons, 1910): "Houses and palaces in Padua were architecturally determined by the fixed boundaries of the continuous arcades linking one house with another." This continuity of line extended even into the ghetto, with its narrow streets and almost Moorish, shuttered windows. The combination of sobriety and joy, of love of order and far-seeking clarity of vision, marked out the horizons of the town. These qualities blossomed in the works of Moshe Chaim Luzzatto, the heir who brought all this grandeur to its final destiny.

THE RAMCHAL'S CHANGING WORLD

In the eyes of the world in general, the Italy of this time was considered past its greatest days. Since the French kingdom had gained strategic control over the country, it had closely assimilated its ideas; and in their new context they gained a new prestige. French cities were built on Italian plans, and French artists returned with new perceptions of light, which they blended into their own environment. Paris began to make discoveries in science based on what it had learned from the professors of Bologna.

It was a relationship not unlike that of Europe and America today; great things still emerged from Italy, but everything depended on French capital and French decisions. The Jews of Italy thus found themselves linked with the principal non-Jewish power of the world, a country that had expelled its Jewish population in medieval times and founded its unity on that act. This departure of the Jews from the lands of the Atlantic seaboard was completed just at the time America was discovered, and thus the Western countries that colonized the New World did so with political forms different from those the Jews had known while they lived there. The mass of Jewry had gone to the East, where they dwelt apart from the developments in science and politics that were to provide them with such new relationships when they emerged from their shelter.

Only Italy and Germany among Western nations, still politically divided, retained small communities of Jews in their midst; there they lived under the internal rabbinic autonomy arrangement known by the term *ghetto*, linked to their neighbors only by the deep-rooted acceptance of the world-order characteristic of the old regime. The beginnings of today's Western culture were stirring around them, Renaissance glories unparalleled since ancient times. In Eastern lands humility was the natural attribute of the surroundings, but Italy was a place of pride, of the arrogant condottiere fighters, of the Medici rulers and those who aspired to their position, of Niccolo Machiavelli, who shaped morality itself to the service of such ends.

It was a more precarious existence spiritually, with temptations of wealth and social preference an ever-present threat; high responsibilities thus devolved on the leaders. In the cities of Dante and Leonardo da Vinci were Jews equal to the task, men of humility greater than the greatness that surrounded them. Their knowledge of true science and philosophy could win over the most confident opposition; they knew what the world around them was doing and also what it would achieve in years to come. The Renaissance spread first to France and then to the countries of the North, providing the forms around which the new Western world developed and grew, and the Torah giants who lived at its source in Italy took on the task of planting a beacon for the day when all of Jewry would enter into that world.

Into this juncture came the Ramchal; kabbalist, poet, playwright, and philosophical guide, leader of a generation tossed by new winds as exploratory thought and voyaging reached out to the ends of the earth. His writings show the influence of their time, the pleasingly abstract quality of Canaletto's paintings and the music of Vivaldi, both Venetian contemporaries, a realism elevated to a world of purer thought. There is no darkness or confusion, but an abundance of subtlety and interplay, coming to final reconciliation. To us they seem startlingly "modern," in tune with the inquiring mode of thought, the researching spirit of those who wish to understand the processes underlying Creation while appreciating their beauty in ways that acknowledge the Creator.

Like Maimonides centuries earlier, the Ramchal was giving his own and subsequent times the intellectual means to sustain them through ideological troubles. He lived in the last generation before the turbulence preceding the French Revolution, and it is remarkable to see the way in which his writings answer every question that revolution would ask. A basis had been laid on which the disruptive events could run their course; works of righteousness had been done that would last forever. But in the story of his life we discern a spirit at grips with forces much deeper even than these: the evils besetting the Jewish concept as such. Thus, we begin to sense what manner of man had been chosen to fight such battles, to build on such treacherous ground.

2

The Ramchal's Youth and Early Influence

The Ramchal was noted as a prodigy in learning from a very early age. From the outset he began to amass knowledge with an alacrity born solely of the desire to accomplish divine service. As his father was a rabbi who had become wealthy in business, he was free from any lack or restraint in circumstances. The way was clear for him to devote his time to Torah, and he was growing up among sages, men who exemplified all that flowed from the tradition of the "wise men of Italy." His first instructor was R. Isaac Cohen Cantarini, a medical doctor who wrote works of rhetoric and poetry. There were also the kabbalist R. Benjamin Cohen Vitali and R. Isaac Lampronti, author of *Breads of Thanksgiving*, one of the earliest systematic treatments of Jewish concepts, but the main teacher was Vitali's son-in-law R. Yeshaya Bassan, head of the Paduan community, who was one of the great scholars of the generation, already famous beyond the borders of Italy. Their relationship was to last a lifetime and beyond, surviving the pains of controversy and exile, never diminishing in mutual respect and love. The teacher set his feelings on record when, after his pupil had first come under criticism, he sent this testimonial letter to the rabbis of Venice:

> While still a young child he came to love the Torah with an affectionate love, and when he grew into boyhood he made for himself a golden coat of modesty, without following things of vanity and the impulses of his heart, the foolish impulses of childhood and boyhood. God gave him sense to listen and to understand, and he was to me like a son. I trained him, I took him into my arms, I taught him as much as I knew, and as I loved him with an eternal love he was on an equal footing with me in my house. I told him every step I made, and all my spiritual possessions were at his disposal, because nothing was hidden from his spirit thirsting after knowledge. And as he used to come to my house every morning, very early, light and swift as a deer, to learn the words of the living God, he searched through all my library, found there some of my writings that God granted me, and also tasted of the *Tree of Life* [of R. Chaim Vital]. Then his mind began to explore in the valley of secrets, and he began to love it with a sweetness of spirit. . . ."

Volumes could not say more; this was the beginning of the path that was to bring him to excel all his teachers in true understanding.

Clearly this was a leader, and he had been born into a time when Jewish leadership was undergoing deep trial and suffering. The upheaval of the expulsion from Spain had sent Jews into desperate plight, and the great men of the time had reestablished the community life in ways derived from the increased understanding of Kabbalah that they had been granted. Kabbalah ideas were being disseminated as never before and were reaching a public longing passionately for redemption, for the dawn of the messianic times.

These ideas originated in true Kabbalah; they were being spread in order to bring about the Redemption; great men had said that the Messiah was indeed ready to come, but the generation was not to be remembered for this. In the mid-seventeenth century, forty years before the Ramchal's birth, events had taken a very different course. The large communities of Eastern Europe had been shaken by the raids of Bogdan Chmielniki's cossacks and the invasion of Polish territory by Swedish forces in 1655. In the West, the turbulence of the Reformation had thrown up sporadic movements agitating for the "millennium," the End of Days, to be achieved by social overthrow. Such were the English Levelers and the Anabaptists in Germany, groups rooted in the peasant uprisings of the Middle Ages. Governments were settling this anarchy with a heavy hand, and homicide had become generalized in countries where Protestants and Catholics lived side by side. Insecurity and desperation spread like wildfire; harbingers were seen in the sky, and numerologists "proved" that the year 1666 would see the long-awaited revelation.

SHABETAI ZVI

The Jews too were ready for ultimate events, and it was indeed not long before the congregants in

the synagogue of Smyrna, in Turkey, were as-
tounded to hear one Shabetai Zvi, the son of a commercial agent who traded in currants to England,
pronounce the Divine Name out loud, a certain
indication of the Redeemer. His fame spread rapidly, mainly due to the efforts of his adherent
Nathan of Gaza. He made decrees, performed
miracles, drawing to himself the passionate hope
latent in all Jewry, without distinction of origin,
wealth, or country of residence. His meteoric rise
took him to the heights of adulation and fame,
galvanizing all Jews to act in unison for the first
time in modern history.

People began fasting and selling their property, ready to move to the Holy Land; the bulk of
the Rabbinate gave their consent, though reluc-
tantly, and even the gentiles began to wonder at
the happenings in their midst. When the Turkish
authorities, alarmed at the commotion, confined
Shabetai Zvi to a fortress, they treated him with
great care, and he continued to receive visitors like
a chief of state. The ministers discussed, they hesi-
tated: was this a true prophet or a rebel? Was the
Turkish state, so long favorable to Jewish interests,
to risk antagonizing such a movement? It was the
summer of 1666, and all were in expectancy of
great events. They could hesitate no longer: let the
redeemer prove himself in the face of the challenge, before matters got out of hand. Shabetai Zvi
was condemned for treason, after a trial watched
by the Sultan in person from the secrecy of an
alcove. Of course he would triumph even over this
. . . but it was not to be. Faced with the death penalty, Shabetai Zvi converted to Islam and was ap-

pointed a "keeper of the palace gates" at a pension of 150 piastres per day.

The entire Jewish world was thrown into consternation; some Jews even adopted Islam to follow their anointed down to the depths from which deliverance had to come. The rabbinic leadership resolved never again to allow such a fever of speculation to spread, and the teaching of Kabbalah ideas fell into sharp disfavor. In England that same summer Isaac Newton, driven from London by the plague, was watching the apple fall in his country garden and drawing conclusions about the power that kept the universe moving in its path. Modern science had gained a degree of purchase on the truth, leaving the Torah bereft of part of its goodwill, the start of three hundred years of struggle and contention to regain it.

It is not difficult to understand the unease with which Jewry was permeated even forty years after events like these. The Ramchal's youthful development was surrounded by the ever-present feeling that Kabbalah represented a tremendous power—capable of saving the world if properly handled and understood, but carrying a corresponding risk if it fell into the wrong hands. In both Sephardi and Italian Jewry, however, the ways of the earlier Kabbalah had become so established as almost to be considered traditional. Rabbi Isaac Luria, known from his initials as the Ari, or "lion," had begun to teach it publicly in the sixteenth century to a few men who became leaders of the population expelled from Spain. Among German-speaking Jewry, though, there was strong resistance to this. The rabbis there were closely attached to a version of the "philosophic" way of life propounded by Maimonides, whose level of learning had been so high that he knew Kabbalah as a consequence of his other studies, without having to treat it as a separate topic. To men of this way of thinking, occupied with the daily exercise of their devolved jurisdiction, the teaching of Kabbalah ideas on their own was like the pulling of a tooth, a shift in the whole balance behind their view of life and practice. After the debacle of Shabetai Zvi, the initiative came into their hands, and they intended to make sure that affairs would proceed in the future on a sounder and more orderly basis.

THE NEW DEFINITION

In this situation the Ramchal's Italian upbringing afforded him the rare chance to gain close knowledge of the Kabbalah tradition from men who had received it in direct line from the original teachers. Elsewhere in Europe at the time, this knowledge was harder to obtain. He listened and asked, understanding more and more, as Bassan was later to tell; by his early teens, he had already outpaced those who taught him. At the age of sixteen, he began to write copiously, thousands of pages on rabbinic topics, ethical discipline, drama, poetry, and Kabbalah. Soon he was widely known in Italy and abroad, and his first pupils began to gather around him. Many Jewish students were attending the medical school, and a select group of them accorded him unquestioned allegiance, showing a willingness to comply with his every wish in the religious manner known as "faith in the wise."

The production of a book was at that time considered a landmark achievement even for a recognized scholar, and for the Ramchal to reach this level at the age of seventeen was a great rarity. Particular delight was shown on all sides that he was choosing poetic forms for his expression; throughout the ages the Jewish people wrote poetry, and the great *tzaddikim* were always producing fine verse. Their works conveyed the heights of the soul's exultation, the lament for the Destruction, and the long exile. Torah concepts could be taught through song, in balladlike forms derived from the entertainments of the country. The Ramchal picked up the Italianate models he found at hand, such as the sonnet, which had already become popular in other languages, but he wrote in Hebrew, harmonizing its spiritual content with the feelings of his time and place.

Works like these had hardly been seen since the early *piyyutim* in Babylonia a thousand years before; many of these had entered the liturgy to be sung at special times and inspired ibn Gabirol and his contemporaries in Moslem Spain.

Both Jews and gentiles in Italy had the custom of producing suitable poems for the "rites of passage," the culminating occasions in their lives. They reminded people of the cycle of existence, linking them with their forebears in earlier times who had "known how to live," and for whom celebration had been an integral part of life's joyful round. In this manner the Ramchal wrote for happy events such as weddings, and the famous "Dedication of the Holy Ark" for the Sephardi synagogue in Padua. There are laments for the deaths of teachers and relatives, reaching anyone who has known bereavement. The modern reader gains an insight into the "golden chain" of life in a ghetto community, with a heightening of perception at his own moments of truth. The author's output showed none of the clumsiness and immaturity that usually mark the works of even great writers in early stages. He began with completeness, and the years that followed tell the story of where he went from there.

As time went by, his life seemed to be pursuing two separate courses, one contending with the tremendous outer difficulties of the era and the other calm and serene, looking both to the past and the future, partaking of an inner peace that bore fruit in written works showing no trace of tribulation or hardship. His theme was the unity of the Torah, the hidden thread of unity weaving together the diverse strands of his life and the life of the world, the secret truth to bring a smile. Padua was his home, Padua saw him moving and heard his voice, and it was Padua that danced at the weddings for which he wrote his song.

3

Poetry and Plays

Over forty of the Ramchal's poems have survived, some in his own hand. All of them were written in Hebrew, though he knew both French and German and probably also understood English, in addition to Yiddish, Judeo-Italian, and the dialect of the Venetian locality. Most are of sonnet length, but a few extend to dozens of verses in epic style; they range from emotional outpouring to deep kabbalistic discourse, and even to intricate riddlelike compositions accessible only to the initiated. On one occasion he lent his talents to the praise of the new pope, which the Jews in Rome were obliged to provide at every enthronement on pain of severe penalties, a rare venture into the world of unpleasantness and power. But, for the most part, his themes are those of Jewish life, peopled by his associates and close family in his town of origin.

When his pupil Elia Concili graduated from the Paduan medical school, the Ramchal wrote a "souvenir" ode for the transition, touching on the emotional points of the event as well as on the finer aspects of the subject's character. Normally this would have been no more than a pleasant compliment, but in the hands of the Ramchal it becomes a form of *mussar*, advice and counsel, as the true spiritual personality is held up for emulation:

> see, those who teach to fools are overwhelmed—
> —those grapes of pure discernment they have planted—
> will they yet heed the voice of understanding?
> noncomprehending, sinners turned astray.
>
> not so for you, my friend; your succored glory
> and fair donations are your mind's own field.
> wisdom and knowledge like a bud indwelling.
>
> healing and seeking like a garment worn,
> and wisdom calling to you in the courtyards:
> "these and all that comes from them will support you."

Certainly Elia Concili was a very special doctor; the lyricism shows us something of the level of delight, the high understanding and moral clarity of the life of this inner circle. Hardest of all for us to realize is that the poet was not exaggerating for the sake of any kind of effect; there really was such a man as Elia Concili, and he did indeed deserve this kind of praise for the efforts he had made. His modesty would also have been equal to the demands made upon it by the publication of the ode. The result is like a beam of warm sunshine pouring into the dark corners of a room; we witness the start of a medical career totally devoid of vanity, cynicism, or professional coldness, something much more difficult to achieve today. The work is different in so many ways from ostensibly similar examples in the literature of the world, in the subject itself, in the way the concepts fit together, in the harmonious relationship between content and musical form. They all build up to something of elevation, a construction of Torah with a message of its own for the soul.

There are hints of many biblical sources in the text, and the last line, in Aramaic in the original, derives from talmudic concepts; but this is still a personal poem, distinct from those with specifically Torah themes. Chief among these is the *"Seder* for Pesach night," which amounts to a "history of truth" from Creation to the Exodus from Egypt. Based on Kabbalah ideas, it cannot be fully understood without an appropriate commentary, but its language alone achieves a matchless grandeur, ably adapting the Italian "victory" mode to depict the Redemption itself. Like all true approaches to God, it ends with prayer but begins with praise for the attributes of the Almighty:

> ruling the world with might, in strength abounding,
> heavenly-dwelling, rock of all our praises,
> stirring in anger like the fire to enter:
> darkness—encompassing, a *sukkah* for us!
> maker of sun and moon, His name repose,
> as sitting by cherubs garbed, our own salvation.
> what man can tell Your praise, Your wealth of powers,
> maker of greatnesses, to whom there is no scale?
> (*Yarim Moshe*, שטו)

One might perhaps be put in mind of a vast, glorious canvas, an Old Master of truth, not one in mere painted images but in words, for the power of the Jew lies only in the spoken word. The eternal concepts are given rhythm and more: a surging immensity, a trumpet call to the inner ear. Though not published in a collection at the time, these poems soon traveled all over Italy by copying and by word of mouth, coming to inspire a large and appreciative audience. Jews in other countries also turned their attention to this Italian source, much as the non-Jewish world was turning to Tasso and Guarini. All through the rest of his life the Ramchal remained known for the breadth and charm of poems like these.

But there were sad occasions as well; mourning is like a revolving wheel that touches every man in his time, and the Ramchal was no exception. In 1730 his sister Lavra Hannah passed away, just as she was to be married. How did one so bound up with eternity really feel such a loss? His elegiac poem gives us clues, but also a sense of bafflement; it is grief, but a spiritual grief, different from that of ordinary people, for the *tzaddik* remains in a bond of trust with his Maker. He picked up his pen to help others who found their world shaken by the absence of a loved one, and he gave of his heart, but his own reaction is still a mystery:

see, my fellows, how the grave-shadow came
to me instead of *chuppah*'s honored splendor;
here was the wedding-house borne to the tomb.
Rachel, O barren, silent one, I called out:
"what is my good but hands full of reward?"
all of my lot has come to peaceful rest

since the exalted Right Hand made her great—
—more than the glory of ten sons, Selah.

This poem, written at the age of twenty-three, shows the mature consciousness of a man old and full of days; when Rabbi Elazar of talmudic times was made head of the Sanhedrin at the age of eighteen, his hair was miraculously turned white in order not to shame those of his elders with whom he would have to sit in judgment. A Jew pledges his life twice every day, always prepared to lay it down, and this world is still a lesser thing than the World to Come.

DRAMA AND STORY

Small written poems had always circulated in the ghetto, but now the Ramchal was given opportunity for a wholly new departure, the bringing of Hebrew verse to the public stage. Renaissance Italy had seen the birth of the theater as we know it today; in the stylized characters of the *Commedia dell'Arte* a form was created, which spread first to France and then all over the world. The stage setting was used to depict "classic interactions," certain conceptual highlights of life or thought, while seeking also to amuse and to entertain. It all answered perfectly to the Italian character and situation: the deep operatic themes, the calculated charm, the view of life as a gamut of human reactions. People could see themselves on the stage, larger than life, less fallible than in reality. There was something of hope in it, some clinging to an ideal world that had perhaps once existed and still lived in a corner of the mind. Many of these dramas had a pastoral setting, harking back to the Greek and Roman classics, with fine verse on the ancient model serving to lull the ear into a reminiscence of Arcadia.

No one would at first connect these escapist fantasies with anything of Torah, yet, around the beginning of the eighteenth century, certain men began to look differently at this medium. They took the theater as a subtle form of instruction, bringing to life a talmudic concept of far-reaching significance concerning the messianic days, namely, that when the Torah was restored to its glory, "the theaters would be turned into houses of study" (*Megillah* 6a). This means much more than just a change in the use of a building; in those days, the halls of study would recover the glitter and allure, the entry to worlds of fascination, which people seek today in the dramatic hush of an auditorium.

Plays on Torah themes began to appear, at first clumsy and imitative, but breaking new ground, creating a public eager to listen by the time the Ramchal turned his hand to this special form. He wrote from the hidden dimension of Kabbalah; realizing how the aspect of entertainment was vital to spiritual uplift, he created sparkling poetic drama, conveying the underlying truths by means of the excitement of dialogue and action. Often the audience would remain unaware of the depth of the concepts involved. He appended a short verse drama, the *Maaseh Shimshon*, to his first publication in 1724, and soon afterward produced his unprecedented *Migdal Oz* (*Tower of Strength*). This title derives from Proverbs 18:10, "the name of *Hashem* is a tower of strength; a righteous man shall run within and be raised on high." It was written for the wedding of Bassan's son and was most probably declaimed from copies by young students in play-reading style, to entertain the bride and groom.

Its allegorical form resembles that of Italian dramas of the period, but only superficially; its real content derives entirely from the world of Torah, with Kabbalah principles to furnish a deep understanding both of the content and of the nature of drama itself. From this standpoint, the world and its events are manifestations of the ten Divine Attributes, the *sefirot*, each of which contains all the others and exists through myriad varied forms in the unfolding of human experience. In order to discuss these concepts, men would give them names with a particular ring of divinity, such as "king" and "princess," "mountain," "sea," and "island." Their interplay conceals the divine purpose; their continuity forms the heavenly plan. When these conversations reach the ear, dormant spiritual faculties are awakened. In *Migdal Oz* the Ramchal constructs a form especially to accomplish this, with a simplicity that goes to the root of understanding.

Though there are many subplots the main plot can be summarized briefly: a story of hatred pitted against love, ambition against hope. In some ancient country, the Eastward Land (the word for "East" in Hebrew also means "original"), there is a tower on the top of a high, inaccessible mountain, the "tower of strength" of the title. No one can reach it and attain its powers, so King Ram ("ex-

alted") announces all across his land that whoever
enters the tower will receive as his reward the hand
of the Princess Shelomit. One day Shalom, the son
of the king of Anamim, passes by the mountain
and, attracted by the tower, investigates its surroundings until he comes upon a cave, whose
entrance is covered with grass. Groping his way
through, he reaches the gates of the tower. They
are partly hidden by stones, which fall off as he
opens them. But he knows nothing of the king's
announcement, and his reward is claimed by the
impostor Zifa ("false") who has secretly followed
in his footsteps.

The king rejoices greatly in the discovery of
the tower entrance and is ready to stand by his
pledge with regard to the Princess Shelomit; meanwhile, she and Shalom meet secretly and decide
to marry. However, Ada, who also wishes to marry
Shalom, discovers their secret and decides to destroy Shelomit out of jealousy. Through various in-
trigues she succeeds in having Shelomit arraigned
before the king on a false charge of plotting to kill
Zifa by sending him poison, unwittingly aided by
her servant and Shelomit's maid. Shelomit is sen-
tenced to die in flames but while her execution is
being prepared, Shalom hears of the fate awaiting
her, hurries to the public square and offers the
king his life for hers. She refuses to accept this, and
in his anguish Shalom suddenly remembers a
verse he had found written behind the gates of the
tower when first he opened them: "If you dare
approach here, the worst in future you may fear."
He declares that the opening of the gates must
have brought this upon him. When questioned by

the king, he recounts the whole story, forcing the impostor Zifa to admit his guilt. Ada asks forgiveness of Shelomit, which she readily grants, and the true wedding takes place. The drama ends with a wedding song by the whole chorus.

Like the stories of R. Nachman of Breslov told a century later in the basic form of the Russian folktale, the play carries a spiritual charge, which is apparent from the outset. This is a story of Creation itself, of the process in life in which one always seems to lose the way on the journey from innocence, through trouble and sorrow, to joyful reunion. Gone are the slyness and elbowing of "romance," the prettified passions of artificial legend. We are left with something that picks out the essential attraction in both romance and artificial legend, dramatizing the secret processes at work beneath the surface to resolve the insoluble dilemma. This element is essential to the story process itself, the desire to be taken out of life for a brief time and to look upon it from a point suspended in the darkness. People strive against evil not through open warfare but by maintaining simplicity, and their trust is rewarded; evil has been created solely in order to try them, before being destroyed forever.

Retribution is handed down in public, contributing in a sense to the idyllic tone of the scenario; the Hebrew verse conveys majestic ideas with force and clarity. This is the private counsel of Shimei, the friend of Shalom, to the young prince:

see how each heart is granted law and precept
lest it go deeper resting in its pride,

fall down to hide in chambers of the belly.
through nooks and crannies will his face be seen,
and he will lack no good from the inspection,
when his desires bow down. . . .

Every portion of the text is filled with concepts of this magnitude and is rich in Torah references like the one here to Song of Songs 2:9; thus, the whole work amounts to a major epic of philosophy. After its early success, the manuscript was lost for a hundred years, Bassan's son having feared to risk divulging it while his friend's controversy was raging; on its eventual publication it achieved even greater acclaim. By that time the Ramchal's cultural model had lost its local significance, and the inner concepts were more prominent.

The Ramchal's era was closer to the primal innocence than our own, though there were indeed famines, plagues, and military clashes. The recent memory of the religious wars coupled with the attempt of the French monarchy to subdue the entire continent scarcely made for a secure view of the world, but they took place within a certain framework of assured truth, a universal acceptance of the Divine Providence, which was shared by the non-Jewish population. Only in the next generation would revolution come, with its ideological roughnecks elevating incitement to the level of an eternal principle. We who are used to living amid relentless change and questioning might see the previous order as unresponsive and even stuffy, and there is no denying that in the case of Italy in the Ramchal's time it had fallen from its previous vigor into a state of lassitude and decline; but while it lasted, it had a link with time-lessness, something that we in our day find hard to achieve. The Ramchal sought to preserve it for us from his vantage point, in the written form that he thought best. Something of the spirit of prophecy still survives in the works of such a man, available to us even through our confusion. We are plentifully supplied with drama, but sameness begins to take its toll; one looks for something from a different world, something with deeper insight into the workings of what we call fortune. The Torah is not just a story, or even a history, but it has elements of both, the elements that speak to us in the language we understand.

GOVERNANCE AND TRIAL

In all this work, however, there was nothing to arouse opposition to the extent that the Ramchal would later encounter. The Kabbalah content here was still on a hidden, allusive level, and he could have continued privately with his deeper studies, in the manner of those who had taught him, without any exception being taken. Even his remarkable youth would not have been held against him. But a Jew must go wherever his knowledge of the present and the future may take him, for wisdom will demand its own increase, being given only to those who possess it already.

There is always a secret dimension to the thoughts of a leader. By virtue of his position he bears burdens of which others know little or nothing. From the height he occupies he can see further than they, and he must still give them the guidance they need to follow the correct path. What leader is free from contention and challenge? People will forget how he earned his place and think only of how he has suddenly become at variance with the principles they consider the most important. A man in charge must guard his counsel. His wisdom alone must guide him, and his humility under heaven, for who is there among his challengers with fullness of understanding? Who can know what it all means without being tested as he has been tested?

And so we come to one of the climactic events of Jewish history, and one of the most enigmatic: the Luzzatto Persecution. The Ramchal was not content to write and teach in the ordinary way; he took it upon himself to act, and his action still arouses controversy 250 years later. Did it stem from the turmoil of Shabetai Zvi, or foreshadow the agitation that would soon surround the chasidic movement? Or was it the concern of a single individual who, having risen high enough to see far into the past and the future, encountered the most elemental opposition as he sought to steer his time toward redemption? We in our generation can only retell the tale as it appears in the documents of the period, for the world in which the events took place had not yet become the world we know. The people of that time had avenues open to them in both love and hate of which we know nothing; a full comprehension must wait until the time when our comprehension itself is finally restored.

4

Kabbalah:
The Holy Society
and Its Opposition

In this period the wisdom of Kabbalah, "true wisdom," was imparted only to the greatest men in each generation. They would study the scheme of Creation and its underlying powers only after many years of impeccable adherence to precept, without disseminating their knowledge more widely. But as time went on and Jewry grew less assured in its ideas, more people began to desire the sustenance offered by this knowledge, and the leaders began to act publicly on its principles, indeed, to discharge their functions mainly by the guidance it offered. It was still a secret, but it was becoming an open secret, and the episode of Shabetai Zvi showed the extent to which the community had become dependent on leaders who could bring it to fulfillment.

The world had been created by speech through the ten utterances "and God said," and this Hebrew speech was still the vivifying element of the Creation. Through the arrangement and pronouncing of the Hebrew letters, holy men could discern secrets and manipulate the order of things in a theurgic manner. This was the "King's scepter," the means provided to servants for the advancement of their Master's cause. Such things had always been possible, though rarely used, but in the Ramchal's time the question of extending their use came to the forefront of attention. The need was compelling, but was there anyone, so late in the day, who could be trusted with these matters? Everything was fraught with danger; a servant who erred could be severely punished, and his public would also be affected. It would probably be wise to show extreme caution. The Ramchal was assuredly wise, but he had embarked on a path seemingly lacking in caution: Kabbalah study in a group setting, under conditions that made heavy demands on those taking part.

Within the ghetto of Padua, the Ramchal began assembling a small circle from among the younger men of the town and the medical school, all close associates of his own. It was called the "Holy Society," and its seven original members put their names to a set of regulations requiring them to engage in study continuously, each member reading a portion in his turn so as to fill all the daylight hours during the weekdays. The study was to be from the *Zohar*, the basic text of Kabbalah, and the members voluntarily contributed the merit deriving from it in order to "perfect" the Divine Presence in the world and thus bring redemption to all Israel. No fixed time was appointed for the men's turns, but each member attended whenever possible, beginning his reading before the other finished, so there would be no interruption.

This method came close to "practical" Kabbalah, whereby the speaking of the holy secrets would move the fundament of the world itself toward the direction the leader had cleared for it. With so much at stake, there were considerable risks; any flaw or demerit in those participating could have highly adverse effects. Thus, the Ramchal entrusted the task only to men of proven standing, one being Isaac Marini, honored in a poem on his wedding, and another, Yekutiel Gordon, a rabbi's son from Vilna in Lithuania, who came to figure prominently in the ensuing conflict and subsequently returned to the north, practicing medicine for many years in Brisk (Brest-Litovsk). The high ethical standards were evident in the regulations to which they had subscribed; they undertook to treat each other in a brotherly way, kindheartedly, accepting remonstrances without anger or hate. Their free gift of the merit accrued was part of the ethos of selfless pioneering.

Soon the circle was extended to include nine more members, among them the Ramchal's brother Shimon, and further regulations were added, including one that enjoined forbearance in the face of "all the mockery of the world." Those who take the path of truth are always exposed to ridicule, but this was a more radical departure, something affecting heaven as well as earth; the nearer a man approaches to God, the more he must answer the heavenly Accuser, and the requirements of conduct increase with every step in that direction. The new members agreed to continue the study all through the night as well as during the day, and other sacred texts were read in the same manner. Every tenth day one member would observe a fast. Those present during the readings were cautioned to "awe and trembling of heart," greeting their teacher and others with blessings for God's glorification and hopes for His help in their service. All the doings of the circle were placed under a rule of total secrecy, never breached through all the investigations.

THE MESSIANIC QUESTION

There was nothing slight or inconsiderable about any of this. All the participants were well-known younger men from prominent families, any of whose doings would be a topic for discussion. In modesty and fear of heaven they strove to avoid bringing attention to their activities, but it was not long before rumors began to spread in the town; soon word would reach the wider public. Yekutiel had become the trusted confidant of the Ramchal, serving as copyist for his writings and acquiring a close association with his purposes. According to the principle of the reincarnation of souls by which a soul may return to the world to complete its destined service, the Ramchal had discerned that Yekutiel possessed a very lofty soul, that of a great sage of former times. He devoted most of his efforts to Torah study, but had kept up his medical work on the Ramchal's advice, having asked whether he should abandon it and been told that it was best to strive from within the world's framework. He was among those to whom the Ramchal had divulged a particular fact concerning himself and the motives behind his Holy Society, the source from which stemmed the changes he intended to make.

It is known in Jewish experience that men on certain high spiritual levels may receive help and instruction directly from heavenly sources. One who received such a "messenger" was R. Yosef Caro, author of the definitive legal code *Shulchan Aruch*, who had been among those expelled from Spain as a small child and subsequently lived in Israel and the Balkan lands. As the generations declined these interventions became rarer, and thus more remarkable, only very venerable men being considered ready to receive one. In the early summer of 1727, however, the Ramchal was remembered in this way; his reaction was one of extreme awe, as he described in a letter to his teacher R. Benjamin Cohen:

While alone in my room, I heard a voice saying: "—to reveal hidden secrets of the Holy King." I rose a little, trembling, and then I was able to strengthen myself. The voice did not cease, but spoke the secret it had mentioned. On the second day I endeavored to be alone in my room at the same hour, and indeed the voice returned and told a further secret. Afterward, it was revealed to me that this was a *maggid* [from the Hebrew "to impart"] sent from heaven to acquaint me with detailed Unifications for my attention, and that it would come every day at this time. I did not see it, but heard a voice speaking from within my mouth. Later it gave me permission to ask questions, and after three months it furnished me with particular *tikkunim* [restorations] to perform each day in order to merit a visit of Elijah the Prophet. Furthermore, it told me to compile a book on Ecclesiastes, concerning what had been explained to me on its contents. Subsequently, Elijah did come to me, and explained further secrets. . . . Souls were also revealed to me, whose names I did not know. . . . All of these things I do when I fall on my face, and I see the holy souls actually in the form of man, as if from within a dream. (*Yarim Moshe*, קי"א)

The *maggid* told him to establish the society, and the prophet also told him that his own soul had originated in that of Rabbi Judah the Prince, known as Rebbe, the compiler of the Mishnah, who had maintained a uniquely close friendship with the emperor Antoninus in Rome, the "wise" emperor who had presided over the grandeur of Pax Romana as the imperial rule reached its peak. All through his life, the Ramchal would carry an echo of this link and of the assertion that in Rebbe had been realized all the qualities befitting the righteous: beauty, strength, wealth, honor, wisdom. . . . He was barely twenty years old when he reached this point, and seldom in all history had one so young been so favored.

When Yekutiel was told of this, he strengthened himself in his devotion, feeling sure that he was in the presence of a man trusted by his Creator.

For three years he kept the secret faithfully, serving as chief lieutenant in the work of the society, and then suddenly he divulged it to another, for reasons that remain mysterious. Would he desert his mentor, revealing a divine matter solely on his own responsibility? Or had the Ramchal decided to take the initiative, feeling that secrecy was no longer furthering his aims? Perhaps even at this early juncture, he had readied himself to face the storms that followed.

THE ADVERSARY

Late in 1729, Yekutiel wrote a long letter to a community figure in Vienna by the name of Mordechai Jaffe, a learned man who was in business in the Hapsburg capital. Addressing him as a man of reputation, he spoke of how it had become proper to reveal to him a portion of the Ramchal's activities and achievements, as much as could be put into one letter. Mentioning the *maggid,* he listed the works that had been compiled at its dictates, speaking of the way in which his own soul-relationships had been explained to him by the Ramchal from this secret source. He implored his unknown correspondent to believe his words and not to compare what he said with the falsehood of Shabetai Zvi, with whom the recipient was believed to have sympathized. He ended with a plea for confidentiality and hopes for long life and peace. The society had been at grips with the Shabbatean tendency in secret, pitting their integrity against its falsehood; the decision to confront it in the open must have resulted from intelligence of a very high source indeed. The *maggid* had given instructions to hold study sessions in a certain way, and now the time had come to put their gains into effect, on carefully chosen ground.

The letter went on its way, cast adrift on the

waters like a note in a bottle. We cannot discern how it traveled after its addressee received it, how news of its contents spread, and how the document itself fell into the hands it did. But with our hindsight, the distance seems short, the route direct and unerring.

Rabbi Moshe Chagis came from a family of fighters: tough, principled men, not given to compromise. He was a scholar of wide repute, formerly residing in Jerusalem, and now rabbi of Hamburg-Altona. His father, Rabbi Yaakov, had upheld the Law during the rise of Shabetai Zvi himself, and the son was a veteran of many battles against the false redeemer's followers. The German port city was a strong base for him; he could organize support anywhere he chose, and he had chosen to fight the ideas of Shabetai Zvi. He believed that his duty lay in casting his weight behind those trends that, thankfully, seemed to be reconsolidating: proper guidance, respect for law and authority, patience in the face of redemption's long delay. He saw Yekutiel's letter, and he saw the enemy in person. A peremptory youth had seized the helm on account of some unverified heavenly agent and was encouraging the promising youngsters to desert the path of reason in favor of . . . what? The secrets were for the Almighty alone; what more did he need to know?

He did not hesitate; he sent a copy of Yekutiel's letter to the Rabbinate in Venice, adding these words of his own:

Mountains of Israel, my teachers and masters, upon you as rabbis and wise men and leaders of the community rests the duty, once you have rent your clothes in mourning . . . to investigate and uproot this wicked company before it propagates its wickedness among the mass of the people, and to condemn all its members as pursuers of Israel. And I myself [by this warning] will have saved my soul. Thus speaks humble Moshe Chagis of Jerusalem.

Chagis felt a need for quick action; he was rooted in his own time, attending to its needs. He fought evil on its own territory, the time-bound world of urgency and restlessness, and this was his disadvantage.

But the Ramchal stood above time-bound contingencies; his purpose would not suffer even if he were driven like a leaf before the wind.

In the meantime, however, his situation was to all appearances highly precarious, with his very standing and spiritual livelihood at stake. The rabbis of Venice had set themselves to their task with determination. Avoiding a direct address to the Ramchal himself, they contacted his former teacher R. Bassan, who was by this time residing in the town of Reggio, calling him to account for his pupil's activities as a man with knowledge of Kabbalah.

Indeed, sir, believe us, that after having read two or three pages of the aforementioned letter our hearts trembled and we said to each other in fear, "What is this that the Lord has brought upon us? . . . Please make this matter known to us, without publicizing it among the uneducated, who would mock at such things . . . or to the gentiles, who would take it as a pretext to attack us.

The fears were in the atmosphere of the times, and who could say they were groundless? Such a danger would call for a stratagem; so the Venetian rabbis appointed the Ramchal's closest mentor as the agent for their investigation. The pull of conflicting loyalties was strong, but Bassan did his best; he became "counsel for the truth," attempting to work his way through the compromised situation into which he had been cast. His pupil was now beyond his actual tutelage, and he spoke to him in more of an avuncular tone, without any trace of legalism or severity. When the Ramchal was told of his prosecutor's identity, he at once wrote to him in person, not wishing to deal by proxy:

> All of us know how hard is strife, and how it is hated by God. . . . Why should we repay Him with evil when He does only good to us? His works and His thoughts are with us for benefit! How will our prayers be acceptable before Him? . . . Dear sir, I beg you to set your heart to words like these, spoken in your ear with great love and from a yearning soul, thus not to give room for the Satan to sport amongst us, chas ve-chalila. . . . (Yarim Moshe, צ)

A "soft answer turns away wrath," and this may even have abated some of the primal force behind Chagis's assault, but did he heed the cautionary words "Beware the hiss of the wise; it is the adder's hiss"? There was no plan, no force compelling him to make a stand. Had he chosen to do so he could have taken a different course, for the human free will is sovereign; the divine purpose would have been accomplished differently. But he judged that he was furthering the majority interest, and the investigation went ahead as before.

CASE FOR THE DEFENSE

Bassan now regarded himself as duty bound to reassure the Venetian leaders, and he placed their qualms before the Ramchal, as gently as he could. Their correspondence traveled to and fro during the early months of 1730, while Chagis endeavored to convince Europe's leading rabbis of the need for a thorough campaign. Already the doubts and fears were crystallizing into an indictment. The true nature of the *maggid* was the main point at issue, along with the Ramchal's general credentials as a man dealing with holy things. He was only twenty-three years old and unmarried, whereas customary practice discouraged the study of Kabbalah by men under forty or without family ties. He had not yet grown a beard, that emblem of holy trust. His description of the *maggid*'s arrival did not seem to preclude the possibility that this was an evil manifestation. What was this "falling on the face"? It was known that there were *maggidim* of higher and lower orders of purity; who could be sure that this one was imparting only the truth? Bassan committed his questions to writing and received replies containing concepts of Kabbalah, in tune with the confidence of their personal aspect:

> It is known to me that I did not yet reach even half the level of the ARI [R. Isaac Luria], in that he was given permission to write [as he chose] but I was commanded to write. . . . He sits alone, and there have also been others greater than I, who have attained to the heavenly Orchard itself. . . . For these matters are not in the individual's providence, but in that of the multitude.

and to R. Benjamin Cohen, also in Reggio:

> I learned [from the *maggid*] things that are not known to
> many, for the concerns of the ARI are of the most hidden. In
> particular, there is the question of how the Infinite One vests
> Himself in this world of Action. The general principles are
> concerned with three things: the divisions of governance,
> the descent of the Light by levels, and the arrangement of
> the luminaries.

The two senior men were won over; R. Cohen
wrote back with warm praise and even guarded
optimism for the outcome. But the opposition was
gaining ground, and the Venetian leaders, described by the Ramchal as "devoid of insight" kept
up their campaign, unconvinced by Bassan's tes-
timonials. They themselves had enlisted his aid,
but his love for his pupil was apparent to all; how
could his appraisal be considered in evidence?

All of Jewish Europe was up in arms. The leadership of Poland, by far the largest community in
the world, had joined issue, spurred on by Chagis's
circulated allegations; some very important people
wanted answers to their questions without any
waste of time. The Ramchal had no alternative but
to defend himself further. In an exchange of letters with Chagis and Chief Rabbi Katzenellenbogen of Hamburg, he kept to his claims, verify-
ing the contents of Yekutiel's original letter in
person for the first time. These claims were very
far reaching; in one letter to Katzenellenbogen he
asserted the authority of "all the members of the
Academy on High," which called forth the strong
support of Bassan to help a delicate situation.

Everyone was setting out his views on the true way in public; multiplicity did not preclude sincerity, but neither did it establish peace. Daily considerations were being set aside and ordinary life suspended in the extremity of the debate.

It all seemed to no avail. Bassan traveled to Padua to seek a solution in person and focused his efforts on the issue of marriage. It turned out that the Ramchal had wished to marry a certain cousin of his some time previously, but her parents had preferred another; on this account he had remained single. Perhaps she had not been the "predestined bride," but Bassan argued against any further delay in seeking out a true bride. Marriage would strengthen the Ramchal in all aspects of his being, and he could not afford to let his enemies continue to exploit a weakness so easily remedied. The time was right; and so it was that in 1731 the Ramchal married Zipporah, the daughter of Rabbi David Finzi from the neighboring city of Mantua, by Bassan's arrangement. They were soon blessed with children, and their union endured in faithfulness up to the very end of their days.

The Ramchal was among those who attached great significance to the linking of the names Moshe and Zipporah; they were those of the Teacher of Israel and his own wife. The lives of people conversant with such ideas remain forever hidden, veiled from the sight of those outside.

5

The Knowing Heart

With the start of married life, the Ramchal entered a period of peace and stability. His adversaries had attacked him more for acting on the instruction of a *maggid* than simply for teaching Kabbalah, but the question had arisen with such force mainly because of the Kabbalah content of his actions. Without this, matters would never have reached such a fever pitch; people were disturbed because of the change in fundamental perceptions, making everything in their lives different from what had gone before. Old adversaries had been laid low, and new ones anticipated, indeed as if heavenly agencies had taken a hand.

Chagis had also been granted his power from above, as the Ramchal acknowledged when he wrote of him to Bassan as "the Accuser," but none of this could impede the true aim, even now when it seemed that the opposition had gained the upper hand. According to basic rabbinic etiquette, it was required of the Ramchal as the younger man to make some move toward appeasing those who had contested him. Peace had to be pursued, and to pursue it he would have to go into a kind of exile, first an internal one, a state similar to quarantine, and finally in earnest. Exile in its many forms was the lot of the entire Jewish people, but on this level of insight it became a paradigm of the people's travails, a state in which constriction and wandering held hidden purposes of restoration. Knowing what was entailed, the Ramchal agreed to back down.

In consultation with Bassan, he signed a document of submission, affirming the rabbinic authority, before a delegation from Venice. He agreed to restrictions on the writing of further books on Kabbalah in the name of the *maggid*, and on using Kabbalah for practical purposes, as long as he remained outside the Land of Israel. The right to teach Kabbalah orally was retained, as was the writing of new books of his own volition. He delivered all his previous works to Bassan as a sign of good faith, and they were sealed in a wooden box before two Venetian emissaries, Yaakov Blilious and Moshe Menachem Merari. An injunction was witnessed forbidding anyone to make use of the works, and the sensitive box was entrusted to the care of Moshe Alprun, a respected elder of Padua. Chagis and the other interested parties received copies of the signed undertaking.

For the moment, all was well; the Ramchal had made no damaging admissions and had safely retreated from a dangerously exposed position.

Even with the curbs on his freedom, he had an opportunity to establish himself in the ways of peace. Accordingly, he turned to writing with renewed ardor, producing nearly forty books and monographs over the next four years. His poetic output continued, but he began to produce what would become the mainstream of his work: the exposition of Jewish fundamentals in belief and practice, in terms clear and simple enough for anyone to understand, but with the deepest and most complex ideas only just below the surface.

"KNOW WHAT TO ANSWER . . ."

No one since Maimonides six hundred years before had applied himself to this task so thoroughly. In the Middle Ages, the revival of Greek philosophical and scientific inquiry had taken place in the Moslem world where Maimonides lived, and it was there that the challenge to Jewish ideas was most closely felt. Ordinary Jews were being troubled by queries based on deep thought; people of quite humble station were fully conversant with the topics of debate. Thus, Maimonides produced works of pure philosophy such as the *Guide to the Perplexed*, and compilations of the facts of the Torah . in forms accessible to the Greek-trained mind.

By the Ramchal's time, however, this deep knowledge had deteriorated; a need had arisen to restate the underlying principles themselves, so great had been the inroads made by the success of the West. In earlier generations science had been relatively crude, a matter of generalization and guesswork along qualitative lines, but during the Renaissance period it became quantitative, acquiring an exactitude with which it overtook philosophy as the main field of investigation. This was the first age of systematization. Linnaeus had arisen in Sweden to count and catalog the forms of natural life, and in France there was Buffon, the keeper of the royal gardens, one of the first men to write popular works on science, of whom an admirer had said, "M. de Buffon has never spoken to me of the wonders of the Creation without convincing me that he was one of them himself."

Coherence and logical clarity had come to the world of inquiry to stay. New sciences were emerging, largely superseding those inherited from antiquity; their ability to classify and categorize, to draw general inferences and specify particulars enhanced life in a world increasingly subdued by exploration and experiment, where communications reached all across the globe and the known outweighed the unknown. This was the start of the Encyclopedic movement, the attempt to construct a universal system in which all knowledge could be interrelated, stored, and retrieved at will. It would not be long before this approach would be applied to human questions, to the working of society and government, of the physical body, and of the mind. The French Revolution produced so many advances by its rational approach, but, in a classic paradox, the use of coherent principles led to doubt and confusion, to the apathy and rawness that surround us today.

Though science was often seen as a challenge to faith, the system chosen by the classifiers was derived from a concept deeper in faith than almost any other: the Tree of Life. It was universally recognized as a truth from within the mind itself that the image of Creation was that of a tree, the four sequential elements of roots, trunk, branches, and fruit representing a pattern to be found throughout the world and its processes. In Kabbalah the truth of this concept, with its connotation of Eden, was explained and understood: how these four elements corresponded to the four Hebrew letters of the Divine Name through which the world was made. This was "true wisdom," able to unify the desire for knowledge with the need for morality, a revelation of sense and order behind the disorder apparent on the surface of things.

Thus, two hundred years after the Ari-zal had produced the first rendering of Kabbalah in a teachable form, this wisdom came out of its retreat. Just as the world began to systematize, so it became possible to provide a view of the Torah and its commandments that would stand this newest test of "faith versus reason." People needed such a view for their Jewish lives, not because their faith was weak or their reason faulty, but because they desired education, a properly formulated truth to take with them into the travails of their working day. Therefore, the Ramchal prepared two classic works, *The Knowing Heart* and *The Way of God*, alike in their derivation from Kabbalah but different in form.

The Knowing Heart (*Daat Tevunot*), published in Padua in 1734, is cast in a question-and-answer mode, a dialogue between the knowledgeable "intellect" and the perplexed "soul" on the workings of Providence. The soul is in a quandary not on questions of faith itself, but simply because it has been placed in a world whose nature is different from its own and told to make its way toward destiny through many perils of doubt and temptation. But the intellect is there to aid its passage, because the intellect has been educated in the Torah, the written and oral sources that have been given to the world to link it with preexistence, the otherwise unknown state whose reality yet dominates our conscience and its predicament.

People are often led to think of faith as something that necessitates abandonment of intellectual claims, a process alien to the rational, self-respecting thinker. Though faith may be the innate attribute of the soul, the intellect in its natural state does not operate by these means; its tendency is to evaluate and compare, to develop by deduction and inference what it will eventually take for truth, rather than to examine the conclusions to which faith of some undefined variety might conceivably lead.

But the Ramchal shows us something very different from this; he selects biblical quotations, which are sometimes familiar, and juxtaposes them in a new way, explaining their relationships in a manner quite unfamiliar to most readers. It is a glimpse of how faithful principles can lead an intellect to develop, to attain heights of understanding undreamed of by those whose knowledge was confined within the created world alone. One might think of this as mere metaphysics, but the human import of the discussion becomes more and more apparent as the work develops.

FACT AND MYSTERY

Certain great questions remain at the back of the mind through the toils of everyday: reward and punishment, Divine Providence, the origin and purpose of life. They are subconscious preoccupations; in a world seemingly so abandoned to the laws of both physical and human nature, it is hard to turn the attention to such things. So much effort is devoted to finding out the patterns and sequences of Creation that they have come to exercise a fascination in their own right, a determination to follow them wherever they may lead. What alternative do we possess? Certainly not an escapist mysticism, but the Ramchal does not take us along such a path. He begins with history: the origins of evil and unbelief. The individual's conduct is the underlying theme, but the individual must first understand the reasons perfection is not manifest and how impairment became the order of the day.

People enjoy the world; they see it as a good place, created on a firm preceptual basis and fitted for life in most senses of the word. Yet the state of it is never satisfactory, and there is not a complete loss of the feeling that it was once better, that natural depredations and the cruelty of man to man are not the eternal order of things. Our envy of the natural and animal states also leads to the conclusion that of all things in the world, the human state is furthest from the perfection it might enjoy. The human being is fallible, but he understands; it is in his hands to improve and repair, as it was once in his hands to destroy. We build up the world that

we inherited, and thus we come to feel how
human fallibility was the original cause of defect—
the concept of the first sin:

> Adam ... possessed knowledge and holiness and every
> noble quality in great degree, being, as he was, the handi-
> work of the Holy One, blessed be He. And being so, his
> deeds certainly shook all the worlds. . . . But note that even
> though he was exalted far above the human species as we
> know it today, he was still susceptible to deterioration, still
> liable to sin and to die, as was indeed borne out by the suc-
> ceeding events. . . . We find, in any event, that man was not
> created complete, but underwent a preliminary lowering by
> the Creator, being created in a lesser state than was appro-
> priate for him, and being subject to further lowering if he
> would sin and be guilty, as was the case. . . . Observe how
> much of cleanliness and of beautiful arrangement He in-
> vested in the creation of man that He did not invest at all in
> the creation of the beasts. And this in the context of . . . His
> doing all in the best possible manner—through the establish-
> ment of parallels and interconnections within fitting relation-
> ships. (*Daat Tevunot*, 184–186)

Providence itself underwent a change to accom-
modate these possibilities:

> It was the providence, then, that was lowered first. Its power
> was weakened and its status and nature lowered, so that it
> no longer created man in the aforementioned exalted state
> but in his lowliness and defectiveness. The crucial factor here
> is that this providence be prevented from creating exalted,
> perfect creatures not by virtue of a deficiency in power (for
> this would not be considered "lowering") but that the im-
> pediment should be outside it. . . . And in the lowering of this
> providence through a weakening of its power, room is pro-
> vided for absolute evil, as we explained. (*Daat Tevunot*, 192)

In today's world the evil is no longer an outside force; it is within us all, having been "eaten"; thus, our statute is that we must "taste" death before our true exaltedness can be realized. This exaltedness, which was once apparent in the body, can now only be reestablished through the medium of our tests and travails in the long passage of personal striving and world history, and it is reestablished through the refinement of the soul:

> The source of the soul is majestic, but the soul diminishes itself in entering the body, so as not to saturate it with refinement in one instant and alter it from what it was created to be. Little by little, though, through virtuous acts, the soul effects the requisite amendment of the body . . . until the body is fit to present itself together with the soul to behold the pleasantness of the Lord and to sojourn in His sanctuary for all eternity. (*Daat Tevunot,* 102)

Here we have the whole expanse of human life, the end summed up in the beginning; but the Hebrew word for "truth" is composed of the first, middle, and last letters of the alphabet. Without the intermediate component we cannot yet lay claim to a complete understanding. In the rest of his discussion the Ramchal explores the workings of the world as we know it, the interweaving of personal and historical factors that form the complete "human condition."

Consequent on these early events, humanity took on a lowered and diversified form, but it still retained something of its primal unity, being descended from a single progenitor. Its state remained like that of one man, whose physical and

intellectual strength wanes as he ages, whose condition is that of illness but not such that he will
die. He is sustained by Divine Providence through
distinct stages of maturity on his progress to the
eventual renewal. The form of this providence also
changes in the course of time, ours being an age
different from historic antiquity as from the
future. These changes are well known to us, yet
little understood in their underlying sense; we still
need to know the intention behind them. All our
lives we are beset by our particular form of necessity; we want to know why:

> The root of all is that the Blessed One desired and willed to
> bequeath of His goodness to the beings that He willed to
> create. And to this end He originated an order of illumina-
> tion and providence proceeding from Him and adapted to
> the level of these beings. . . . What the Blessed One desired
> in this providence is that it constitute a providence of holi-
> ness itself, emanating from Him. . . . But because He willed
> the existence of this lowly world He likewise desired that His
> providence be of a lower order. . . . This is certainly demean-
> ing to it, for it was not originated for this purpose. It emerges,
> then, that the lowly, earthy aspects of His providence that
> we witness constitute a diminution and demeaning of the
> providence itself. But thus it was conceived in the Blessed
> One's mind—to cloak His providence in these dark forms until
> such time as it will strip itself of these vestments and appear
> in its pure, clear form. . . . The Blessed One has fashioned
> great causative mechanisms and cycles for the attainment
> of this end. Thus the root of the variation in the world's times
> is . . . God varying this providence from ascent to ascent until
> it arrives at its essential form. (*Daat Tevunot*, 154)

What we see in the evils of the world is a mask-
ing of their true situation:

Evils . . . are kept within bounds by the power of God's decree, and constrained by His command not to grow in strength and blot out what exists but to obtain in such degree and bounds as is necessary to establish the character of existence. And they are so adjusted as to grow in strength at such times as such intensification is needed and to diminish in strength when necessary, all as dictated by the needs of the time in accordance with the decree of the Supreme Will. The result is that there are certainly imperfections and defects in nature, but they are not so great as to blot out the Creation. The evils are so attuned, however, as to ultimately intensify to the degree in which its objects will be obliterated (for all that exists is destructible) and their existence hangs on a very fine thread within the fabric of the Supreme Wisdom. (*Daat Tevunat*, 158)

Thus, the world is set for both choice and destiny, with many occasions for the individual to grow in faith as he sees the evils become more and more rampant. The Ramchal's formulation takes on an echo of the life of Italy, where the immediate choice is set in the context of the long-term view, that of a kind, humorous people carrying on their struggles down the generations as the empires rise and fall in vanity. It is a perspective from the center, the springboard of all the life that bustles down from the north and along the sea. Such a way of life might be termed "philosophical," but here it is more than that: it is faith in action, endowed with the power to reach conclusions, with the warmth of true knowledge like a fire for the shivering traveler. One sees the world as a home, not a chaotic jungle where the next danger will come from some wholly unexpected quarter.

THE MORAL MAN

If the Torah confers the ability to deduce the facts
of nature, what will become of science? Its goals
come within the Torah's scope in a general sense,
part of the intellectual equipment of the truly wise:

> One who superficially observes the constituents of this cre-
> ation will, in the beginning, find them to be scattered and
> separate, that is, not all conjoined to a single end, but each
> one an entity in itself, serving its particular end. . . . For there
> are so many elements among the inanimate objects, among
> the vegetative, and among the animate, that . . . each one
> must have been created for its own purpose, and all of its
> aspects must serve for the attainment of its particular end
> and for nothing more. With all this, one cannot fail to notice
> a hierarchy of levels in nature, and if one . . . began from the
> heavens and worked downward to the nethermost depths
> of the earth, reflecting all the while upon all of the creations,
> he would find all of them appropriately scaled one beneath
> the other. But he who probed further in wisdom would find
> all of the creations interconnected in a solid bond . . . con-
> taining a multitude of creations and a profundity of orders . . .
> for at this point wisdom must branch out and probe infinity
> to know the function of every creation and its place in the
> universal intent. (*Daat Tevunot*, 194)

The sweep of these statements brings us far
beyond the gropings of the deductive method.
How would science have proceeded had these
things been known? Darwin observed the animals
to be fitted for self-preservation, but he could not
relegate the universe to a swarming chaos; he
needed a hierarchy, even an anarchic one. The eco-
logical viewpoint gains access to the fineness of the

world's balance, but it still stops short of transcending the idea of "system function," the assertion that natural processes remain self-contained. Any single conclusion loses its force once it is elevated into an ideology, running the risk of disproof; for the very scientific method that selects and isolates processes runs counter to fullness of understanding. The uncertainty principle arrived too late to change habits of thought so long ingrained, but it helped to readjust the perception; after the two and a half centuries of scientific work since the Ramchal wrote these words, many people are arriving at a "holism" only one step short of his first observations. That step is the biggest of all, the "leap of faith," and the Ramchal shows the place at which it occurs:

And in truth you will see that even in His acts there is no evil in the world except in elements in isolation, prior to their being considered as contributing elements in a complete process; but there is nothing complete that is evil. . . . When this completeness is supplied, what is evidenced is certainly good . . . with the fulfillment of the prophetic assurance (Isaiah 12:1), "I will thank You, God, for Your anger against me." (*Daat Tevunot*, 196)

Though science does not claim to encompass moral truths, it inevitably enters moral territory, especially where the origins of the world are involved. Questions of true purpose enter through the back door, once the methods of science gain ascendancy. Causation can play tricks on the mind, and not all scientists are careful enough to acknowledge the fragility of their causative edifice.

When the Ramchal speaks of causation, it is in the context of the ordinances of the world's governance, as by a king, and of human endeavor as a form of service that the king has decreed:

> Our sages have said (*Sanhedrin* 37a), "A man must say, 'For my sake the world was created,'" and explained, "R. Simai said: 'This is analogous to a tall rock standing at the crossroads and causing the passersby to stumble. The king commands: "Chip it down, little by little, until the time comes when I will remove it from the world."'" (*Daat Tevunot*, 140)

This is the eradication of evil, a charge on each man to achieve, first from within himself and subsequently from the entire creation, in order that the human race, the goal of Creation, should attain to its true harmony. In this connection the Ramchal speaks at length of reward and punishment, and of the institution of *mazal*, the inexorable, heaven-guided unfolding of events that seems to override the human free will and conscience:

> Because the Holy One, blessed be He, truly desires the complete perfection of the universe and the complete removal of evil, He desires to conduct Himself with the righteous according to the ordinance . . . whereby their righteousness will not avail to spare them from the sufferings of this world. And this is certainly not within the framework of reward and punishment but only within that of the universal perfection being realized by way of them. (*Daat Tevunot*, 308)

Wisdom of this kind gives an opportunity to see deeper into the world around us, discerning connections not apparent at first sight:

Only this we know: there is that in the essence of the Creation the perfection of which requires increase and diminution. This is the nature of the twenty-eight "times" mentioned in Ecclesiastes 3 ["a time to build, a time to pull down," etc.] corresponding to which there is a witness in the heavens—the moon, the waxing and waning of which images this concept. And there are profound understandings in this regard possessed by those who are wise in the ways of the moon and in its relationship with the sun in all of its states. (*Daat Tevunot*, 312)

History appears completely different from the Ramchal's perspective, with the human fate a fusion of two concepts apparently impossible to reconcile. All our days we live out this paradox, but the Ramchal puts it into words:

For the Creator . . . established two ordinances: reward and punishment, and *mazal*. And He is the decisor, sometimes resorting to one and sometimes to the other, in accordance with His knowledge of what better furthers the good of His universe. . . . For if the Creator always only afflicted the righteous, this would still be a test for free will, but not a very great one, for they could console themselves in the knowledge that they were unquestionably righteous in that they were interminably afflicted. And any sensible person would gladly suffer these afflictions, for they would be confirmation of his righteousness, the wicked not being afflicted in this manner. But the Creator desired an area of greater trial, in which . . . on the surface of things the ordinance seemed to be (Ecclesiastes 9:2): "All unto all, one happening to the righteous and the wicked." . . . For it is impossible for anyone to plumb the depths of what the Holy One, blessed be He, is doing with him. . . . And in everything there is an aspect of both (reward and punishment, and *mazal*). (*Daat Tevunot*, 316)

In this exposition we see the complete plan displayed before our eyes; we are warmed instead of intimidated, as the most dire contingencies of the world are handled so as to seem explicable, part of a beneficent scheme for the bestowal of good. The author constantly smiles, as each turn of his phrasing reveals another hidden benefit, another delight for the understanding. He picks out the thread of unity behind the most diverse facades, investigating yet always maintaining his true precepts. It is a work for the man to whom knowledge is as essential as bread, for the seeker after truth, undeceived by appearances and not ready to accept a mere assertion.

6

The Way of God

In *The Knowing Heart* the Ramchal depicts the outlook and standpoint of Jewish thought; his detailed analysis of the distinctive concepts in themselves is reserved for the companion work *The Way of God (Derech Hashem)*. In lucid Hebrew he arranges them in an order of great formal beauty, as if to make a garden of trim hedges and lawns, a spiritual Versailles, out of the seemingly wild and random scene that meets the one who delves straight into the works of source. In his introduction to the book, he speaks of the value of systematic thought in the process of comprehension: not to confine the mind, but to provide association and connections that gratify the intellect, prevent it from tiring, and give it that sense of well-being associated only with completeness. In his day this was a great advance, and there were learned men who feared for the fullness of understanding, and even for the work ethic itself, if such satisfaction could be obtained without toiling through the sourcebooks from the outset. The author was widely criticized for publishing both of these works; it was said that a man so young should not have compiled works of such scope and authority, especially with a basis in Kabbalah. With hindsight, however, we see that the decline in capability had been such that people could not have achieved the required level in the time available to them. This in itself was a sign of how close the redemption really was and how clearly the Ramchal had discerned the stage to which his own times had developed.

The Way of God begins with discussion of the divine scheme on a deeper level, focusing on the particular role of the Jewish people. Why was it necessary that they exist as a separate nation with distinct tasks and relationships? How did their special character originate?

The human race initially had a chance to permanently regain its original [pre-Adamic] state and rectify the spiritual damage that had been done. The proper procedure would have been for the roots and heads of Adam's descendants to first elevate themselves to the rectified level. Once this was accomplished, both the roots and their branches would remain in this state forever, since the branches always follow the roots.

The time provided for generations to function as roots, however, was limited. During this period the gate was open and the opportunity existed for any individual to properly prepare himself and permanently become a good and worthy root. . . . According to the Highest Judgment, it turned out that none of them deserved to rise above the degraded level to which Adam and his children had fallen as a result of their sin. There was, however, one exception, and that was Abraham. He . . . was chosen by God as a result of his deeds, and . . . enabled to produce branches possessing his characteristics.

The decree, however, was not that the other nations should be destroyed. It only meant that they would have to remain on the lower level that we have discussed. This lower state . . . came into being in the first place as a result of [Adam's] sin. These nations still have the human aspect . . . and God desired that they should have a counterpart of what was actually appropriate for all mankind. . . . They were thus given commandments, through which they could attain both material and spiritual advantages appropriate to their nature. These are the seven (universal) commandments given to the Children of Noah (Genesis 2:16, 2:24, 9:3–7). (*Derech Hashem*, 132, 134, 136)

THE DIVINE PLAN

Abraham's descendants were thus those to whom the Torah was given and among whom the Land of Israel was divided. All Jews subsequently born derive from them as primary branches, thus fulfilling the obligations of divine service accepted at that time. These accomplish the final rectification of the world from its lower state, by the linking of physical reality with holiness above, which was established at the time of the giving of the Torah. Through this link, our actions, speech, and thoughts in this world acquire a different significance when they conform with the Torah's requirements:

Devotion in general consists of two elements: study and observance. . . . The study of the Torah has a very important

function in man's perfection. . . . Among the Influences be-
stowed by God . . . there is one that is higher than all others
and whose essence is more excellent and significant than
anything else that can possibly exist. This is the ultimate
counterpart of God's essence that can be found in creation. . . . This Influence was bound by God to a concept
created specifically for the purpose of sharing His glory and
excellence with His handiwork. This concept is the Torah.
The ultimate aim of this concept is realized in two ways,
namely recitation and comprehension. God composed a
combination of words and sayings to constitute the Five
Books of Moses and on a lower level the Prophets and Writings. He then bound this highest Influence to the words of
these books in such a way that when they are uttered, this
highest Influence is transmitted to the one reciting them . . .
[also] through the content of these words' true meaning the
Influence is transmitted to the one who comprehends them.
It is obvious that the higher the level of comprehension the
higher will be the corresponding Influence derived through
it. . . . [However] to a greater or lesser extent virtually every
Jew has access to this highest Influence. (*Derech Hashem*,
238, 242, 244)

This aspect of study leads to practical conduct,
the action and observance required in so many
spheres, in each of which there are choices to be
made. Thus, there are both positive and negative
commandments, actions to be performed and
others to be refrained from; some relate to circum-
stantial events, some are periodic, and some are
continuous, such as the love and fear of God:

When one stands in awe before God's greatness, he is purified of the darkness associated with his physical body and is
enveloped by the Divine Presence. . . . The highest level of
this is when one attains the ability to constantly experience

this awe. . . . This is a very difficult level for people to fully attain, but to the degree that one does attain it, it has the power to purify and sanctify him. This is particularly true with regard to one's observance of God's commandments and study of the Torah, since it is the one necessary condition for their perfection.

Love is the thing that binds and attaches man to his Creator, increasing his spiritual strength and enveloping him with an aura of the Divine. The main element of such love is the joy in one's heart . . . and the devotion of all one's powers to sanctify God's name and fulfill His will. . . . Also included in this general category is belief in God and particularly trust in Him. (*Derech Hashem*, 352–254)

With these means it becomes possible to approach closely to the Divine, constantly gaining in understanding and kindness. The positive commandments take on the character of an occupation, surpassing worldly effort in importance. Prayer in particular ceases to be the preserve of desperate moments and becomes a constant channel for human need and aspiration:

We must realize that God gave man the intelligence to function in this world, as well as the responsibility of caring for all his own needs. This concept is founded on two principles: the first involves the significance and importance of man himself . . . and the second is based on the fact that man must be involved with the world and bound to its various aspects. . . . Although this is a worldly rather than a holy path, it is what man needs during this period of his existence, according to the general order. . . . Though it was necessary that man be lowered to some degree in this manner, it was also imperative that he not be lowered too much. The more he would become entangled in worldly affairs, the more he would darken himself spiritually and divorce himself from the highest Light. God therefore prepared a remedy for this, namely, that man should initiate all worldly endeavor by first bringing himself close to God and petitioning Him for all his worldly needs. He thus "casts his burden upon God" (Psalm 55:23). (*Derech Hashem*, 284–286)

TIME AND ITS CHALLENGE

In this manner the weekday round becomes goal oriented, no longer left to function mechanistically without thought for how material striving came to have so much significance in our lives. Similarly the weeks and seasons of the year do not consist entirely of working days; some are set aside for spiritual purposes entirely, to make a distinction between what is required for the world and what is reserved for the purposes that lie behind it:

> The concept of time was therefore arranged so that it should contain certain days of worldliness and days of holiness. . . . It was further decreed that days be set up in a constantly repeating cycle, consisting of a specific number of days. The designated number was seven, since all existence was created in seven days, and therefore every element of its being is included in this number. . . . It was determined that the end of each cycle be holy, and this elevates all the other days. . . . This was a great gift [the Sabbath] that God gave to Israel because He desired that it be His holy nation. It was not given to any other nation, since its benefits were neither appropriate nor appointed for them. (*Derech Hashem*, 312–314)

Sabbath observances enable man to strengthen himself to receive this benefit, following in their details from the particulars of its holiness. On a lesser level are the observances associated with the festivals of the year, such as Passover and the New Year (Rosh Hashanah):

> With the Exodus from Egypt, the Jews were set aside so that they would have the opportunity to purify their bodies and prepare themselves for the Torah. In order for this to be possible, they were commanded to rid themselves of leaven and eat *matzah*. Bread is designated as man's primary food, and it is therefore precisely what is required by the state that God desired for man in this world. Leaven is a natural element of bread, making it more digestible and flavorous. This is also a result of man's appropriate nature, since he must have an urge to evil and an inclination toward the physical. At a particular determined time, however, Israel was required to abstain from leaven [since it essentially stems from evil and decay] and be nourished by matzah, which is unleavened bread. This reduces the strength of each individual's evil urge and inclination to the physical, thus enhancing his closeness to the spiritual. (*Derech Hashem*, 320)

Today's world is greatly changed from that which existed before the Exodus, when God's name was not known in the world and the redemptive observance of the Torah was not mandatory. Our providence follows from this change, and we are now the possessors of an order whereby we can attain to merit. We can rise from level to level, constantly perceiving renewal in every detail of the world. On the New Year the entire world is re-created, as God comes to judge it in the scale of merit, according to processes known to us in their main principles:

At this time, the Accuser is prepared to prosecute mankind for its sins. . . . The attribute of Justice does not allow any good to come to an individual if he does not deserve it. This very rule of Justice, however, gives rise to the principle that certain deeds should have the power to abate strict Justice. . . . One such concept is included in the teaching "When one disregards his own nature [not retaliating when another wrongs him] then God disregards all his sins." This is also part of God's "measure for measure" judgment. The heavenly courts thus act toward him with mercy, but this itself is ultimately a result of the attribute of Justice. This, however, is only one of a number of things that the Highest Wisdom decreed should be repaid in this manner, another such concept being the sounding of the *shofar*. Israel was commanded to sound the *shofar* on Rosh Hashanah to bring forth the attribute of Mercy, and when they observe it correctly it has this result . . . to remove power from the Accuser, and finally to place themselves in a position so that God should make use of His superiority and direct things with His sole authority to disregard sin. (*Derech Hashem*, 324–326)

Periodicity and special times form a framework within which we live, but we also know our situation in general through the events that make up the bulk of our days, the contingencies occurring throughout life itself. We strive for food, clothing, and other necessities; we are involved in social contacts, the fabric of relations that we ourselves call reality:

There does not exist a single concept in the world, whether it be a process or circumstance in anything that exists, that is not set up and ordained according to what must exist to fulfill the purpose of Creation discussed earlier. In order that it be attained completely, all these details must exist within the limits in which they were actually placed. . . . Commandments were therefore given for the various aspects of all these concepts, in order to place them on the side of the good rather than on that of evil. . . . If the limits [defined by these commandments] are not observed, such activities remain on the side of evil. They then result in the spread of corruption and pollution, as well as the spiritual darkness that decreases the highest Illumination. . . . This is the basis of the blessings ordained by our wise men for all worldly concepts and pleasures. (*Derech Hashem*, 330–332)

This philosophical realization is the keynote of the Ramchal's study: everything in a Jew's life contributes to his role in the better founding of the world and the furtherance of its true aims. Eating the permitted food, marrying within appropriate horizons, bearing children or mourning the dead, he can unite speech with intention, create a unity of thought and deed. This is not the way of boasting or fanfare, in the Italian or any other style; glory is a private thought and humility a fact of life as simple as a smile.

The Way of God quickly gained worldwide popularity, which it enjoys to this day; it is a treasure house of concepts, common to all approaches in Jewish life, studied anew by men of learning for its freshness and logical appeal and by beginners for its informative simplicity. It finds its place in moments of respite, ready to encourage and strengthen as it enters into the fiber of being.

7

Worldwide Controversy and the Move to Amsterdam

Ostensibly the Ramchal's situation during this time was secure; he had become a father, and he continued to benefit from the success of the family's business enterprise. His heart was linked with the life of the community around him, as his poetic output continually showed. The Holy Society was still in existence, no longer pursuing the aims renounced under the written agreement but functioning as a private circle for the study of Kabbalah in the manner of general learning. This in itself was not objectionable, but all the same, it did not find favor with the rabbis of Venice. Over the months and years, they set out to gather wisps of information from spies, compiling a dossier that was a monument of insubstantiality. They suspected the Ramchal of nameless offenses, of some violation of the spirit of the agreement he had entered into, without ever formulating a charge.

Chagis himself was concerned to see the agreement prove effective in stalling the Ramchal's purposes, and all the information that came to Venice was forwarded to him. It was not long before the Ramchal found out what was happening on his doorstep; as early as 1732 he wrote to Bassan of the worsening of conditions:

> There is here [in Padua] one wicked man, a complete joker, who has made it his business to write every week to someone in Venice. His name is Chaim Rosanes, and this wicked man writes exclusively what Evil puts in his mouth, without any grounds at all. And when it reaches Venice, the news at once spreads all over the city, to that imbecile Blilious, and thus to R. Nehemiah Cohen and the others. How can one stand against such things?

No man, however elevated, could escape the pain of such slander, even though the instigators were unimportant people; "life and death are in the power of the tongue," and the Ramchal was suffering mercilessly for the callousness of others. There was indeed no defense. He had to carry on his life and work in the knowledge that moves were afoot to afflict him further. Only in prayer could he find release, through the personal means available to anyone in anguish; to those who have witnessed the holocaust of our own times, his words have a prophetic ring:

> Give peace to those of Your flock who are poor, since they are of the aspect of King Messiah who is poor and destitute, as it is said: "Judah (the ancestor of Messiah) went into exile through poverty."

When (a man) stands in his strength, then he is called Man; but when he descends (through poverty), it is said of him: "and a man visits, that he should not rest overnight" and he becomes like a beast. From this aspect Israel become like a flock, as it is said: "coming like a ram to the slaughter, like a ewe silent before the shearer."

Thus, their blood is spilled like water, and they are like beasts standing to be killed. This is a sacrifice on Your exalted altar, but at the time when Your unity will be revealed upon us, they will say, "He who spills the blood of man, by man will his blood be spilt."

And the word "blood" when completed (by adding one letter) becomes "Adam," Man. . . . Master of all worlds, we will be fulfilled by Your oneness in truth. Complete in us the image of Man, and manifest Your salvation. Lord, do not delay. (Prayer, תמה)

A man can be poor in the midst of plenty, never knowing where his sustenance is coming from, trusting only in the Almighty. Feeling such trust, he can even elevate his own poverty to the point where he experiences that condition in a general sense, realizing the extent of the deprivation of others better than they themselves. Such is spiritual victory; the battle against opposition is the battle with oneself, the struggle to remain a thinking and feeling human being against the desire to be neither. As long as the lips can move, a person is still connected with the Creator; the Ramchal prayed out of his knowledge, the wisdom he had gained on behalf of his people, so that others could maintain that connection as their own efforts began to slacken. His chain of pleading follows the development of a single thought, and the crucial element in the reasoning is supplied by Kabbalah: the addition of a letter to complete a word. Without this link in the chain, coming as if from nowhere, the redemptive process cannot begin; the argument would turn around on itself, endlessly waiting as hope began to dwindle. But when the goal of all these disparate contingencies comes in sight, it cannot be reached except through the secret content of the Torah. As the wheel of fortune turned, it reached a point where the bulk of the people began to realize this element in themselves, and they looked to their leaders for the elucidation and teaching that the times demanded.

THE LEAP OF FAITH

The Ramchal was ready and equal to the task. He wrote to Bassan of the new turn that his work had taken:

> Now I am writing another work, which I began only a week ago. . . . The first portion is a selection from the words of R. Shimon bar Yochai chosen to refute the arguments of a philosopher. . . . In truth it is a considerable labor . . . sorting out the wisdom for such a mixture of holy and profane. . . . I hope to have it printed in Amsterdam, where there are those who have affection for me . . . and thus the thing will meet with success.

This work was the famous *Hoker u-Mekubbal*, the dialogue between a philosophic thinker (*hoker*) and kabbalist (*mekubbal*). It set out a plan for the extended public teaching of hidden Torah that has influenced its dissemination ever since. Only by this means could worldly arguments be refuted in a manner that gave moral satisfaction; here and in the books that followed, the Ramchal drew openly for the first time on the treasury of symbolism in the Kabbalah to answer those who saw the world solely as a natural phenomenon. He depicted the principles of Kabbalah itself in language anyone could understand:

> The secret . . . is the attributes of Kindness and Judgment, since these are the prerequisites for reward and punishment, Kindness operating in inwardness (the soul) and Judgment in outwardness (the body). This in general is how the Infinite One contracted His light and how it became a discernible operating factor. Kindness and judgment themselves resolve into "right" and "left" respectively, as into the aspects of "face" and "rear," and of "male" and "female."

The presentation was geared to the love of logic prevalent at the time, and it was a time when mathematics generally would make its decisive leap into the realm of a coherent discipline. New relationships were mushrooming all across the universe of thought—the fruits of Newton's calculus and the advanced algebra of Lagrange. Who could speak to men like these of the ancient wisdom of the Jews, the way of obedience where understanding follows upon action? It was hard for anyone to maintain a footing amid such rapid change, let alone for Jews as yet untaught in the deeper thinking behind the Torah they knew. Following the talmudic caution "Know how to answer the freethinker," the Ramchal entered the debate with pamphlets that circulated all over Europe, arousing controversy wherever they went.

According to the Ramchal, it was time for a major change in methods of instruction, time to supply the "missing letter" that would lead Jewry to the messianic time; but for a man already the center of a full-scale investigation, this was easier to say than to do. As with the controversy over the *maggid*, his new ventures in print brought a storm of protest from official quarters. The rabbis of Venice, acting on behalf of like-minded men in every Jewish center, began to inveigh publicly against the Ramchal, accusing him of flagrant acts of deviation calculated to undermine the interest of all right thinking Jews. He was prepared to remain silent, serene in the trust of his leadership; but when the attacks were public, there had to be a response of some kind, if only to avoid the worst consequences for the concepts themselves.

Bassan also had not been spared calumny; he was accused on the basis of "information received" of having opened the box of documents and returned some to the Ramchal. Still pursuing his role as referee, he wrote to the Venetian leaders, a stark decisive statement designed to leave them under no illusions as to what they were dealing with. He set his own views forth, describing how he had authorized the Ramchal to publish his controversial *Hoker u-Mekubbal*:

Over an interval of two years . . . he composed a work, and he set it before me for my inspection, lest there be found in its phrasing anything that might run counter to God's kingdom . . . and I found in it no defect whatsoever of that kind.

... His secret writings are hidden from us ... and we can judge only what we can understand. ... These books themselves are withdrawn and sealed from the eyes of us all, being no less than the murmurings of exalted fury and passion. (Yarim Moshe, רלב)

The candidness of these statements must have startled the opponents more than anything thus far in the controversy. The teacher had come out in the open, saying that his pupil's activities were indeed as earthshaking as had been alleged, but that neither he nor they could do anything to stop them or contest their propriety. It was a "showdown"; all they could do was accept his word that the Ramchal could be trusted, even to these lengths, far beyond the normal rabbinic "checks and balances."

The leadership itself was at issue: would Jewry go down the path of public Kabbalah for all, as the Ramchal was advocating, or remain guided by those great books that had formed its thinking in time past. The Ramchal was not in dispute with the early writers. He felt that their successors were no longer capable of applying their instructions, especially in changed circumstances, and he was ready to stand and act alone in order that a new and different view should prevail. It was one against the majority, a situation in which the lone voice should generally be made to accede, but the Ramchal was claiming more than just a divergent view. With his close teacher to back him, he was invoking the great concept of the "leader of the generation," the one overriding voice of truth in the times; this was the principle, as old as Jewish life itself, that had led Joseph into dispute and contention with his brothers. And this time, the strife took place in the shadow of Shabetai Zvi and seemed to the Venetian leaders another appearance of the same menace in a more refined and intellectual quarter.

INDICTMENT

When it became known in Venice that the *Hoker u-Mekubbal* was ready for publication, the Rabbinate prepared to act decisively. While the Ramchal was in the city for a short stay, he was visited by three cmissaries, rabbis Blilious, Merari, and Gabriel Paduvani, who handed him a written ultimatum in formal terms. The demands were that he cease teaching Kabbalah even to his own pupils, that he take an oath not to publish any work of his own without the permission of the Venetian Rabbinate, and that he sign a new undertaking incorporating these demands. Though the Ramchal was still willing to stand by his agreement of 1730, these new restrictions could not be accepted in the same spirit. They were demeaning in tone, a breach of etiquette generally; in particular, he pointed out that Padua did not fall under the Venetian jurisdiction in such close personal matters, implying that the Venetians were using the strength of the ruling power to force their side of the issue. This ran counter to the principle of Jewish self-determination as the ghetto autonomy enshrined it, and the Ramchal refused to sign. It was an open challenge, on the dual ground of leadership and personal

Torah integrity; henceforth, no holds would be barred.

The accusations took on a wild character, stepping outside the bounds of trust normally accorded by men of learning. It was a story of libel and fabrication. Blilious testified, in his ignorance, that he had found formulas "for commanding the Satan" among the Ramchal's papers in Padua, and even "black" instruments for this purpose. Bassan explained the true meaning of the formulas; when Blilious brought a man to corroborate the evidence, he was unable to do so, but the damage was done. Other spies spoke of mysterious visitors to the Ramchal's house, and letters written years beforehand by Yekutiel Gordon were distorted so as to imply trafficking with impure powers. It was a struggle for power, a stooping to any level in order to discredit the Ramchal.

Bassan began sending messages to the other main communities of Italy: Mantua, Ancona, and Livorno. Helped by the Ramchal's father-in-law, R. Dovid Finzi, he organized protests against the Venetians, encouraging the leaders to write to the Ramchal himself for explanation. Both men affirmed that they had backed the Ramchal in publishing the book in question, supporting his right to publicize his views. They were two men against the massed ranks of Europe's rabbis, but they fought strongly to bring the uncommitted members over to their side. Meanwhile the Ramchal continued to send them indications of the level that his work in Kabbalah was reaching; letter after letter came from Padua describing revelations never before made public. How could the cause of such a man ever be said to fail, no matter what events might lie in store?

But in Chagis, they had engaged a strong adversary. He wrote to Venice from Hamburg, urging the supreme penalty for heresy: excommunication from the body of the Jewish people. Declaring his view that anything less would open the way to a "second Torah," he consigned the Ramchal to the fate reserved for the impure in heart. Such was the saving power of Kabbalah that it thus aroused the ultimate in opposition, until only through silence, the "thought that is higher than speech," could the truth still be discerned.

Though the conflict had its origins in true Jewish debate, it had by now gone far beyond the limits of such things. The Ramchal had taken on a bigger fight, the biggest of all; he was pitting his self-sacrifice and the strength of his knowledge against evil itself; he wanted to break the power of the "Other Side" and see Jewry through peril to its destiny, its tryst with the Creator. He was taking the responsibility of revealing things hitherto regarded as secret; why should he do so? Why should knowledge of them not continue only among the mighty few?

The Ramchal had his standpoint in timelessness; born in the country most closely characterized by time, by continuity, he had striven to reach the eternal. Once he came to his universe, he had a matchless opportunity to look down time's corridor, into the future as well as the past, and to do what would be most felt as the generations and the centuries rolled on. He saw the start of modern science and how science would come to dominate history, confining the emotional spirit as it spread, first within the countries untouched by progress, the Eastern lands where most Jews then lived, and finally, as those countries broke into fragments, to the inner levels of the heart itself.

An era was emerging in which there would be no room for secrets. Nature would be raided for its content, the treasury of thought piled high with facts that had hitherto been allowed to function undisturbed. And this habit of thought soon would spread to human affairs; politics would come to be regarded as an exact science and people as inherently perfectible, if only they would yield their privacy to the greater good. The French Revolution would sweep all before it in its claims, exacting higher and higher payments of loyalty and greater and greater penalties for treachery. The secret police would rule, not only within the court as before, but among the general population.

There were to be no secrets. A ruler would have to be all knowing; to know all, he would need to find out everything. A succession of tyrants would rise, starting with the relatively well balanced Napoleon, but soon turning uglier until the final horror was revealed—the brief reigns of Hitler and Stalin. The millions whose lives and homes would be strewn across the landscape by the grasping hands of these men and the faceless ones who did their work would fall victim to a cruel twist of a development once seen as the start of a dawn in human happiness: analytical thought replacing the patchwork inherited from the Middle Ages. Medicine and psychology would lay bare the heart and mind. There was to be no more muddling through. There were to be new ways and new men; there was to be industry.

THE WAY TO THE FUTURE

Wherever industrial development took root in the world, it brought with it an increasing need for controls. Watt's steam engine developed the existing machine to the point where it ran faster than a man could move. How was it to be controlled? He invented the centrifugal governor and was able to let the engine accelerate to a pace where it could power factories, move hundreds of people across the country, with no more than cursory attention. As the machine age established itself, it began to demand political controls, to harness an often dissident people to the new ways. In former times the rhythm of the seasons had been all that was needed. People were bound to the soil and its demands, no more thinking to abandon natural cycles than to dispense with seedtime and harvest. It was all heaven sent. But the new controls were manmade, with a human propensity for oppression as indeed for failure.

To the Ramchal this process was all the consequence of exile, of Jewry's separation from its land and the Torah that was at home there: the sundering of mankind from its life-giving roots, the oppression of the tyrant. He wrote of how the world progressed to good by means of evil and the work of subduing it, knowing from the unity of Torah how everything in creation is made for benefit. He could help to fulfill this purpose; if he publicized the secret Torah among Jews, he could create a new level of privacy and integrity for mankind, an awareness of Divinity that no worldly circumstance, however ugly, could touch. Once Jews had a basic knowledge of Kabbalah they would possess a new home, a place from which to reconstruct what the world in its course was bound to shatter. And so he studied and prayed, wrote his works, and trusted in heaven.

The opposition he encountered came from men who feared internal upheaval that might prove more damaging than the turmoil outside. Would it not be better to maintain the Jewish world in its separation, to stop it from being eroded, than to risk everything in a total reconstruction? Who would ever keep pace with it? No one could tell them they were wrong; no one but the Ramchal himself. He did according to his light, and he was bitterly fought, but the outcome was never really in doubt. For the individual would rise above the invective and the lies, and the facts themselves would speak in the final judgment.

There was no process by which the two sides could be reconciled. Each was compelled to strive at the limit of his strength, endeavoring to create for the other facts that could not be ignored. As the extent of the Ramchal's activities became clearer, Chagis and his associates tried to strengthen the existing order into something with qualities of permanence. They were the leaders; they had exercised their responsibilities without demur for many years, fighting against the heretics to the greater glory of God. They were great thinkers and commentators in their own right, not men whose opinions would count for nothing.

But in the great tidal movements that underlay the wanderings of the Jews, their world was already being sapped by the forces of change. The future was beginning to take shape, and it lay not in the lands of the East where Jewry had flourished since the medieval expulsions, but in the Western sphere, in the burgeoning colonial countries and their holdings across the sea. By the start of the eighteenth century, the communities in those countries had found their feet and were looking to their wider position in the Jewish world. And the center of their life, the chief lodestone and hub of their system, was the city of Amsterdam.

When the Dutch completed their struggle for independence from Spain, they began to expand their seafaring activities into formerly Spanish preserves, creating a new prosperity for themselves based on the Protestant ideas then struggling for life. In their eagerness to counter the power of Spain, they were quick to offer refuge to the Marranos, the Spanish Jews who had hidden their religion from the Inquisition and suffered so much at the hands of thoroughgoing Catholic zeal. With Jewish enterprise at the heart of their trading city, the Dutch built a strikingly vigorous empire across the world, supporting satellite Jewish communities in every part. India, the Caribbean, Brazil, and the North American colonies soon harbored tiny Jewish settlements, each contributing to the central emporium with the highly prized tropical goods that flowed through its hands. These

Jews were the forerunners of the life we know to-day; in Amsterdam, where the ghetto had never taken a restrictive form, they exercised an intellectual as well as commercial influence on those around them, out of all proportion to their numbers. The freedom of association brought Rembrandt into the Jewish houses, to discuss ideas on his own level with the luminous minds that he found there; he was not alone in coming to seek them out.

Though the Dutch power in the Americas soon succumbed to the rise of the British, they still held a bigger stake in the Far East, then the main axis of seaborne trade. In the 1730s their volume of business was such as to draw in the produce of even the British holdings themselves, so that Amsterdam's position as the port of entry for the whole Continent was largely unchallenged, as that of Venice had been within the enclosed maritime world of the Mediterranean. In this happy symbiosis, the Sephardi Jewish life flourished as never before. A string of Jewish settlements in Europe and across the world was looking to Amsterdam in spiritual as well as worldly matters, with the dawning perceptions of life in the West to be shaped and guided, formed into the very foundations of Western Jewry today.

THE AMERICAN WAY

The early "Jewish Pilgrim Fathers," who had come to New Amsterdam under Peter Stuyvesant, became established members of the British colonies.

No longer compelled to struggle for their very existence, they settled in the other colonies, Philadelphia and Rhode Island, and built the first synagogues. They shared the anxieties of the other colonists: the fear of Indian raids and of attack by European powers, the awe at the immensity and plenty of the new land, the struggle against the harsh climate and the hazards of travel. What was it like to be a Jew in such a place and time? They were still fully observant, as abandonment of the faith had not yet become the price of emancipation; but they were out of contact with their roots, short of books and of good counsel. There was as yet no coherent Jewish framework for their lives, no leader to whom they could turn in the certainty that he would understand their problems.

On their journeys to and from their chief city, they examined the need for such a leader; a man fully familiar with Western ideas, a man of surpassing stature and merit who could encompass within himself the vast expanses in which they had come to dwell. It was not surprising that when the Ramchal began to look beyond his native Italy for refuge he should think of Amsterdam as the place most likely to make use of his services. The Sephardim were accustomed to the ways of Kabbalah and needed a man who knew how to put it into practice.

No one was any longer in doubt that pressure on the Ramchal would increase to the point where he would have to leave not only Padua but Italy itself. This was exile, from the town of one's fathers and from a land where Jews had lived uninterruptedly since the time of the Roman Republic. Rabbi

Nachman of Breslov explains how lands of ancient Jewish residence enter into the category of the Land of Israel, exile from them being an aspect of the separation from the true abode. For the Ramchal too, there was physical desolation to be considered. The family business had ceased to prosper, due in part to the circumstances around the *tzaddik* himself, and the burden of maintaining the entire family had fallen on his shoulders. He had to go where he would find real opportunities, as well as a friendly atmosphere in which to function spiritually.

When Amsterdam began to show a willingness to accommodate him, he made his preparations for the move. His younger brother traveled ahead, to prepare the ground and to arrange a settlement with the community. The Ramchal was offered an unpaid position as head of the *yeshivah*, effectively the chief religious authority of the town; a master was provided to teach him the craft of lens-grinding, an industrial mainstay that was largely in Jewish hands and sending exports all over the world. By these means, he would be able to establish himself anew, the better to accomplish his purposes in the Jewish universe, striving for redemption according to the way he had chosen.

How close he must have been to this goal of existence is hinted at in a letter from Yekutiel Gordon, written in confidence to R. Solomon Zalman of Venice in 1730. The pupil related that the Ramchal had composed an entire new Book of Psalms, also numbering 150; they would be sung in the hour of redemption itself when the psalms of David were no longer necessary. The psalms of today are expressed in the "feminine" mode, compared in the sources of Kabbalah to a lioness; in the future will emerge a "masculine," triumphant mode, that of a lion. The Ramchal had been able to render the unparalleled change into actual chapter and verse, written on paper with a physical pen. His manuscripts had been among those consigned to the "box" in 1730; there were few who knew of their existence or their true import.

When R. Solomon Zalman revealed it to his colleagues, they were up in arms. The Ramchal was to be stigmatized forever as a heretic, for daring to pretend that writings of the present era could supersede the psalms of King David himself. He was accused of presenting his works to confuse the people by pretending that the Redemption was at hand and that his writings should henceforth be the only true Torah. Ignoring the Ramchal's achievement, as well as his restraint from publicizing the psalms at all, they proceeded at once to their judicial conclusion.

On 5 *Marcheshvan* 5496 (1736), a ban of excommunication was published against all the Ramchal's books, though not against his person, to be read in every synagogue the following Sabbath. It branded the composition of psalms for the future time as heretical, consigned them to be burned, and pronounced penalties against anyone who helped their author. Thus, almost every gateway was closed to the Ramchal, leaving hardly a hope that the ban would be ineffective in any of the countries where Chagis and his associates ruled.

EXILE

But by this time he had already left Italy for good. On the twenty-third of *Cheshvan*, 1734, at the very end of the traveling season with an ever-present threat of snow, he and his wife, with his children, father, and brothers loaded their belongings and set off to the north, to the Brenner Pass that provided the way through the encircling mountains. It was the day after the Sabbath, probably the last full week of the year in which they would have a chance of getting across the Alps; after they left, the winter set in, with its confinements and its resort to store. Those they had left behind would have many hours in which to ponder the meaning of the flight of Moshe Chaim Luzzatto.

To travel from the Adriatic to the North Sea at that time was a considerable undertaking. After the journey across the Alps, the whole of Germany had to be traversed with its poor roads, the exposure to the weather, and the risk of bandits. They went slowly, only venturing across open country in favorable conditions, staying with the Jewish communities along the road. In this way they came to Frankfurt-am-Main, the "Jerusalem of Germany," in the early summer of 1735, weary from travel and hoping to recover their strength for the last stage. However, it was here that the hand of Moshe Chagis finally descended on the Ramchal, more harshly even than before.

Without warning, the Ramchal found himself summoned before a rabbinic tribunal presided over by the chief rabbi of the city, R. Yaakov Cohen.

Chagis had sent him all the details of the case, and he was ready to bring matters to a head. He told the Ramchal that no authority in Europe would tolerate further activities of this kind, insisting that he renounce them entirely. Far from his home and his destination, faced with the hint that he would not be allowed to travel farther, he felt that "the Accuser had gained the upper hand"; there was no alternative but to comply. A document was presented and he signed, later confiding in a letter to Bassan that he had been under duress. He had done his part; the Almighty had His own designs and would complete them in His own due time.

The leaders in Venice still felt, however, that the difficulty had not yet been resolved. They turned their attention to the group of the Ramchal's close associates still remaining in Padua and to Bassan, demanding that they surrender the box of manuscripts, which had been sealed in 1730. Bassan knew that this would mean perusal or destruction of the documents and refused to comply. The opponents reacted strongly; Chagis even wrote to the Reggio community officers over Bassan's head. Bassan wrote to the Ramchal, by now in Amsterdam, of the pressure he was feeling; the Ramchal replied that if it was causing too much unpleasantness, he was prepared to have the contents burned under Bassan's supervision. Under the strain of so much mutual anguish, it was finally agreed that the box would be taken to Frankfurt and delivered to Rabbi Cohen, who would then decide what to do.

The fate of the box then entered the realm of legend, with rumors that it was intact in several localities, and even that a certain widow in the city of Prague had had the copy of the psalms in her possession. In recent times, a letter from Rabbi Cohen was discovered, which described what had befallen the box and its contents: some of the manuscripts were destroyed, and the rest were buried secretly in a damp spot known only to the rabbi and his two assistants. It was a decree from on high. Whatever the truth may have been, what we know is that all that remains of the Ramchal's writings is like the pieces into which the Tablets of the Law were shattered on Mount Sinai. Not until the Redemption will we be able to understand the heights of his thought; we must accede retroactively to their return to the kingdom of the unknown.

What clues do we have to his true aims? By the time he left Padua, he had reached the point where he felt able to speak out on the nature of life as a whole and of the way in which a man should walk. Characteristically, for himself and for his time, he did so in verse, with the secret quality of song to support his words. In forms chosen from Italian literary models he had written the "Life of the Shepherd," one of the last Paduan poems; it brings out some of the deepest concepts of Jewish thought, reaching to the pure counsel of the Psalms and the Song of Solomon. Deep as its yearning may be, it is not for some distant future or faraway land, but for something within the bounds of human possibility, "near to you, in your mouth to do it":

if man were but to qualify his heart
and no more to desire, but only lead

his sheep towards a welling water-spring,
then from their breasts alone would he derive
sweet milk to drink, between their ready rows—
how good his lot would be! as duty-bound
to happiness, since if the wheel would turn
and turn about, no murmur would escape
his lips, no hurt be his,
but that our life is woeful short in span.

fresh springs would greet his eye, and there ahead
between the rock-clefts they would softly run;
to ferret out their source he'd never move.
the sun would turn and turn, but he would never
meditate on how it holds the course.
sweet music would he play, and in among
his sheep would walk the vigor of his soul.
each grass-blade he'd discern, but never how
it sprang from nothingness into his view.
only in his Creator will he now
repose belief, and serve Him all the day;
never to seek the hidden, or bring out
a covered thing to sight.

8

New Horizons and
The Path of the Just

It is written in the Talmud that a man should live in a city of recent settlement, because its sins will be few. By the norms of the period, the Jewish community in Amsterdam was new, hardly more than a hundred years old. In 1735 its air had a freshness, an expectancy, in more respects than just the bustle on the crowded wharves. The Ramchal's arrival was greeted by the Jews with eagerness and joy; no longer on the neglected fringe of Europe, they had in their midst a man who at the age of twenty-nine was by far the most prominent figure in the spiritual world, whose every concern was a matter of weight and moment in all places where Jews came together.

He settled down with his family, each of whom was made welcome in the city; his father especially was treated with great kindness because of the hardship of his dislocation, but he later re-

turned to Padua for personal reasons. The Ramchal wrote to Bassan when the winter came, urging calm now that things had become more settled
and stable.

> Thank God all the learned men here come to visit me and
> assemble in my house whenever they can spare the time.
> They wonder why I refuse to teach them True Wisdom [Kab-
> balah], but it is not because of the Frankfurt undertaking.
> . . . Now please set your mind at rest and do not trouble your
> pure heart by pondering on my case. . . . If the matter will
> not be known to us in this world, we shall know it in the
> World to Come. (*Yarim Moshe*, רמג-ה)

His reluctance to teach Kabbalah came from
a desire to leave controversy behind, to seek out
peace and privacy in order to study undisturbed.
His duties were minimal, and he could be happy
that people were coming to him from all over the
new Sephardi Diaspora, not always to meet him
or to ask questions but just to be near him, to carry
on their lives under his protective wing. He was a
shield to his generation, a "tree planted by the
waters." When he wrote to his pupils in Padua who
had suffered so much on his behalf, it was with
words of personal comfort:

> My brothers and friends, may peace be upon you. . . . Know
> God's purpose in this world. . . . Be of good heart, and keep
> far from gossiping and lies. . . . As for me, I am walking here
> among friends, studying the Torah with them, and my heart
> is turned to God. (*Yarim Moshe*, רמה)

Even here, though, his opponents tried to un-
seat him; they sent spies to keep watch and tried

to foment an agitation in the city, but it was becoming apparent that the onslaught was spent. No amount of slander could prevail against the transparent righteousness seen in the Ramchal by all who came in contact with him. Soon his merit was firmly established, and the opposition exposed for what it was. The victory was as complete as ever in the history of Jewish controversy; in Frankfurt, Rabbi Cohen had collapsed and died suddenly just after burying the box of documents, and his passing had reduced the opposition altogether to silence.

The Ramchal was free to pursue redemption, earning his bread with his own hands. It was an opening of a new world, a world soon to be known with scientific exactitude; we can gain some understanding of what it was to be a pioneer of thought at this time by a glimpse of the developments taking place in the science of the world itself, the field of geodesy.

THE KINGDOM ABOVE
AND THE KINGDOM BELOW

With so much excursion into new lands and seas, it was inevitable that the navigational arts be a scene of great activity. The Parliament of England had offered the famous Longitude Prize for a reliable means of determining an east-west position, and in Paris that same year, 1736, the Academy of Sciences had turned its attention to the problem of the true shape of the earth. Was it oblate, flattened at the poles, or prolate like an egg? The academy mounted a major expedition to the far north, to Arctic Sweden, one of the first ever undertaken purely for scientific discovery, in order to find out by measuring the "arc of the meridian," the length on the ground corresponding to a degree of angle.

Pierre Louis Moreau de Maupertuis and his party set up their base at Tornio on the Gulf of Bothnia in the early summer of 1736. They established a series of triangulation points stretching out to the north on mountaintops overlooking the forests, hauling their massive surveying instruments through river cataracts, engulfed by swarms of flies. An angle-measuring zenith sector, three meters wide to ensure maximum precision, had to be carried to the top of Mount Kittis, north of the Arctic Circle, and was used for star sightings just as the winter began to close in. The river was freezing behind them as they returned to Tornio, and once it had done so, they used the flat surface to measure their base line. In the polar darkness, they worked on by the light of meteor showers reflected from the whiteness of the snow:

Judge what it must be to walk in snow two feet deep with heavy poles in our hands, which we must be continually laying upon the snow and lifting: in a cold so extreme that whenever we would taste a little brandy, the only thing that could be kept liquid, our tongues and lips froze to the cup. (Oral Report to the Royal Academy of Science, Paris, 1737. Translation London, 1738)

For their hardships they had the reward of being the first to answer one of Europe's burning scientific questions; the discovery of the oblate

earth made possible every map and chart that followed. As they strove on the ground, so the Ramchal was striving in the Torah, to chart the course
of the Jews; though he might be in his home in
Amsterdam, the sacrifices required of him spiritually reached a degree far beyond that of a scien-
tist working in the Arctic night. He had set a new
direction for himself, one that encompassed and
surpassed the ideals of the rabbinic opponents to
his Kabbalah. He was ready to prove that he could
serve the purposes of individual life and conscience like any great leader of the past. To this
end, he wrote the work for which he is today most
widely known: *The Path of the Just* (*Mesillat Yesharim*), studied in every place where true Jewish ideas
are handed on.

To open its pages is not merely to consult a
work of reference. It is an entry into a world of
concepts greater and more influential than those
encountered elsewhere, a world whose challenges
and rewards grow in understanding with every
step along the way. The author himself provides
an analogy to guide us in this entry, a conceptual
model drawn from the Italy that was his key to the
pathways of the world:

> To what is this analogous? to a garden maze, a type of gar-
> den common among the ruling class, which is planted for
> the sake of amusement. The plants there are arranged in walls
> between which are found many confusing and interlacing
> paths, all similar to one another, the purpose of the whole
> being to challenge one to reach a portico in their midst. Some
> of the paths are straight ones that lead directly to the por-
> tico, but some cause one to stray and to wander from it. The
> walker between the paths has no way of seeing or knowing

whether he is on the true or false path, for they are all similar. ... He who occupies a commanding position in the
portico, however, sees all of the paths before him and can
discriminate between the true and the false ones. He is in a
position to warn those who walk upon them and to tell them,
"This is the path; take it!" (*Mesillat Yesharim*, 40)

This defines the role of the leader in Jewry,
the "faithful shepherd" as Moses was termed; he
constitutes the restoration of the Temple toward
which he guides those who take his counsel:

He who has not yet achieved dominion over his evil inclination is in the midst of the paths and cannot distinguish between them. But those who rule their evil inclination, those
who have reached the portico, who have already left the
paths and who clearly see all of the ways before their eyes—
they can advise him who is willing to listen, and it is to them
that we must trust. (*Mesillat Yesharim*, 42)

The "portico" of this illustration as yet only
exists within the hearts of the righteous; once a
man has made the journey to the *tzaddik*, to see
him and hear his counsel, then his life begins to
take on a pattern of restoration and repair, his
actions becoming directed to that end. The Ramchal describes the *tzaddik*'s state of being; only
through understanding the nature of the journey's
end will a man ever come to start upon the road:

One who is holy ... and clings constantly to his God, his soul
traveling in channels of truth amidst the love and fear of his
Creator ... such a person is himself considered a tabernacle,
a sanctuary, an altar. ... There is no question that what was
brought up upon the altar was greatly elevated because of

its being sacrificed before the Divine Presence, elevated to such an extent that its entire species throughout the world was blessed. . . . In the same way the food and drink of the holy man is elevated and is considered as if it had been sacrificed upon the altar. . . . In accordance with this view, anything at all that is made use of by them in some way is elevated and enhanced through having been employed by a righteous individual, by one who communes with the holiness of the Blessed One. (*Mesillat Yesharim*, 328)

Thus, we come to understand why it is that in our time when the Temple is destroyed, it is not enough to learn holy things from books alone. One must seek out the righteous in person, in order fully to understand how they live among us and how to benefit from their contribution. The chasidic custom of holding great public gatherings around the rebbe, and especially of sharing his meal, is an example of this course of action; when a man makes himself into an instrument of the divine will, then the very act of approaching him acquires a new significance. To prepare oneself to receive his teaching is a process in its own right, requiring a new understanding of life and relationships; new depths become visible, perception changing constantly under the urgency of the divine spark that lies within every Jew.

This preparation is progressive, arduous, and intricate; the Ramchal analyzes for us the process through which a man comes close to God through ethical discipline. Even for us today, its counsel serves as a guide to holy things in general, an extensive view of how the world of truth emerges out of the world of necessity, error, and confusion. The talmudic master Rabbi Pinchas ben Yair first laid down the basic "progression" of how one trait is acquired, which then leads to another. Everyone is taught that "cleanliness leads to godliness," but there are more stages than that; the cleanliness is really a spiritual accomplishment in its own right, and for godliness to follow upon it requires a special approach not so readily understood.

LADDER TO HEAVEN

However, it is the study of relationships as they exist in the Torah that most of all serves to implant the desired aspirations in the mind. There are five principal modes of divine service: "love," "awe," "wholeheartedness," "observance," and "walking in His ways." All of the Torah, written and oral, is concerned with these and their details; the Ramchal rose to the peak of his mastery of Hebrew prose style in describing them:

The fact of the matter is that true divine service must be far purer than gold and silver, as David says about Torah: "The words of God are pure words, silver purified in a crucible upon the earth, refined seven times." One who serves God in truth will not content himself with little in this respect and will not consent to take silver mixed with dross and lead, that is, divine service mixed with impure motives . . . for one who does not cleave to God with true love will find such purification extremely tedious and burdensome. He will say, "Who can endure it? We are earthly creatures, born of woman. . . ." Those, however, who love God and desire to serve Him will rejoice in showing the steadfastness of their love for the Blessed One and in strengthening themselves through refining and purifying it. . . . And as Scripture explicitly states (Proverbs 23:26), "Give your heart to Me, My son." (*Mesillat Yesharim*, 206)

Worldly inclinations tend to pull one away from this goal, until they come within the control of the individual versed in these concepts. To enable people to subdue their inclinations, the Ramchal analyzes humanity with psychological fineness of touch, as here in the famous discussion of anger:

There is the furious man, about whom it was said (*Shabbat* 105b), "If one becomes angry it is as if he serves idols" . . . for he is bound by nothing but his anger, and he will go where it leads him. . . . There is another type, far removed from the first in degree of anger . . . who will not become enraged over every lack of conformity with his will, small or great, but when he reaches the point of anger, he will become greatly enraged and give vent to his wrath. . . . This too is unquestionably evil, for much that is very damaging may proceed from him during his fit of anger, and he will not afterward be able to straighten what he has made crooked. (*Mesillat Yesharim*, 160)

From this unhappiness, however, the author proceeds to a more congenial human climate, where anger, once defeated, appears in its true value:

There is another . . . less inclined to anger than the aforementioned type. It is very difficult to arouse him, and his anger is neither destructive nor all consuming but mild. It lasts no more than a minute, the amount of time it takes from the

awakening of anger within him to the awakening of his understanding against it. . . . His is certainly a good portion . . . for
our Sages have said (*Chullin* 89a), "The world endures only
through him who bridles his mouth during a quarrel." (*Mesillat Yesharim*, 162)

These insights leave nothing to chance or guesswork; we see the Ramchal's hand like that of a
gardener, parting the leaves gently as he appraises
the need of his plant. Once these ideas are assimilated, the whole world seems a different place,
gardenlike in its variety of scene and path. It is a
matter of perspective; to small creatures, everything can seem overwhelming, tangled and chaotic,
a "tale told by an idiot," as Shakespeare was almost
content to conclude. But the Ramchal sees from
above, like a giant; once he takes us on his shoul-
der, we also see from a better angle, and after we
are set down, we find that we have grown in the
process. We know a little of his heart, feel how
deep is his understanding of mortal trouble and
pain:

Hate and revenge, too, are very difficult for man's spiteful
heart to escape, for in view of his being extremely sensitive
to insult and suffering great anguish because of it, revenge,
being the only thing that will put him at rest, is sweeter than
honey to him. Therefore, if it is within his power to abandon
the urging of his nature and to overlook the offense so as
not to hate the one who ignited hatred within him . . . if he
can do this, he is strong and courageous. Such conduct is
easy only for the ministering angels among whom the aforementioned traits do not exist, not for "dwellers in houses of
clay whose roots are in dust" (Job 4:19). (*Mesillat Yesharim*,
140)

"TURN FROM EVIL . . ."

The Ramchal's sovereign remedy is the study of the Torah, to enhance the latent human urge to good, and he takes the opportunity to show great truths of the mind as it comes to approach its true fare:

> Very often even after one has resolved to be fastidious [in avoiding errors] he is liable to wrongdoing in certain areas because of their not having come within the province of his understanding. For a man is not born wise, and it is impossible for him to know everything. But in studying these writings, he will be awakened to that which he had not recognized, and he will come to understand that which he had not previously grasped, even such matters as he will not find in the treatises themselves. For when his mind is alive to these things, it will survey all within its domain and bring forth new understandings from the wellspring of truth. (*Mesillat Yesharim*, 174)

This view of education stands in strong contrast to the Western ideas of culture and of technical prowess. Does the reading of sonnets and plays make one a better person? Can Shakespeare help in the decisions of life? And when a man can build a house or a car, can he thereby build his own heart? What is the true goal of attempting to improve oneself, to rise above the level of the beast?

If a man were to advance thus far along the Ramchal's path, he would certainly have made great strides in understanding, but his progress would not be complete. From here on, the author concerns himself with the positive commandments, with "doing good" as opposed to the first

stage of "turning from evil"; it is here that he
stands forth as the navigator, guiding with his
hand on the helm. Here is the decisive change in
life-style, the entry into truth as a way rather than
an entity; this is the challenge to the understanding for those whose ideals still turn in the direction of our world rather than toward the reason
for which it was formed:

> If you look more deeply into the matter, you will see that
> the world was created for man's use. In truth man is the
> center of a great balance. If he is pulled after the world and
> is drawn further from his Creator, he is damaged, and he
> damages the world with him. And if he rules over himself
> and unites himself with his Creator and uses the world only
> to aid him in his Creator's service, he is uplifted and the world
> is uplifted with him. . . . As our Sages have said (*Kohelet
> Rabbah* 1:36), "This world is like the shore and the World to
> Come is like the sea." (*Mesillat Yesharim*, 20)

Here is a meeting of East and West, a balance
between the desire to use the world and the urge
to leave it all behind. For this is the need of the
soul; when a man lives in conformity with his
soul's promptings, he acquires in this world a fore-
taste of the soul's delight in the World to Come.

In the second half of his book, the Ramchal
explores in depth the traits of the pious man himself, known in Hebrew as *chasid*, from the word for
kindness. The idea of the *chasid* runs through Jewish life from the earliest times; he shows consideration beyond the actual letter of the law, with
God and with his fellowmen, extending the influence of God through his own efforts into as many
areas as possible. Unlike the nations of the world,

the Jews are given active commandments, things to do that take up time, effort, and money and help to form a personality rooted in the satisfactions of work and service. This active role is not always understood, and there are many misconceptions stemming from the confusion concerning the service of God and the demands it makes on men:

> A consideration of the general state of affairs will reveal that the majority of men of quick intelligence and keen mentality devote most of their thought and speculation to the subtleties of wisdom and the profundities of analysis. . . . There are few, however, who devote thought and study to perfection of divine service. . . . It is not that they consider this knowledge unessential; if questioned each one will maintain that it is of paramount importance and that one who is not clearly versed in it cannot be deemed truly wise. Their failure to devote more attention to it stems rather from its being so manifest and so obvious to them that they see no need for spending much time on it. . . . It has reached the stage that when one sees another engaging in saintly conduct, he cannot help but suspect him of dull-wittedness. . . . The result is that saintliness is construed by most to consist in the recitation of many psalms, very long confessions, difficult fasts, and ablutions in ice and snow—all of which are incompatible with intellect and which reason cannot accept. (*Mesillat Yesharim*, 2–4)

What then are we called upon to do? If the intellect rejects these common notions of piety, in what way does it find a purchase on the subject? The answer is that behind the basic guideline provided by the written commandment itself, we have the strong and far-reaching concept of the hint, the pointer toward the underlying wish of the one who gave the instruction. We are not unthinking machines but men, possessed of thought and feeling:

> We notice at all periods and at all times, between all lovers and friends—between a man and his wife, between a father and his son, in fine, between all those who are bound with a love that is truly strong—that the lover will not say, "I have not been commanded further. What I have been told to do explicitly is enough for me." He will rather attempt, by analyzing the commands, to arrive at the intention of the commander and to do what he judges will give him pleasure. The same holds true for one who strongly loves his Creator; for he, too, is of the class of lovers. (*Mesillat Yesharim*, 216)

Through this love, the *chasid* becomes his Master's representative in the world, carrying His honor and reputation along with his own. He seeks out a teaching that will educate him in the practice of beneficence and mercy to all living creatures, with the many detailed distinctions that life can pose in this respect. Without this knowledge nothing can be achieved; the sages of the Mishnah laid down as a basis for this activity that "an uneducated man cannot be a *chasid*," meaning that there is an essential realization through Torah, particular to each man, that he must somehow learn and that will raise the whole way in which he relates to the divine imperative. Once this is achieved, through the counsel of the wise, his life in Torah can be said to begin.

Purity, humility, separation from worldly things; these are the universal concepts of saintly conduct. What makes the Ramchal's understanding of them different from that of others? Many men have counseled solitude and meditation, extoled the lowly over the vaunting and proud. But it is in his finer distinctions that we catch the special insight that will give us the clue to his position:

> What must be understood is that actions should not be judged for saintliness at first glance, but should be carefully observed and reflected upon so that it may be determined how far their results extend. For at times an action in itself may seem worthy of performance, but because its results are evil, one will be obliged to leave it. . . . This decision is left to an understanding heart and an honest intelligence, for in view of their innumerability, it is impossible to consider particular instances. (*Mesillat Yesharim*, 268)

The faculty of action is always the key concept; the view is of thought united with action, the thinker and the man of action never coming into conflict, as human frailty is perpetually at the center of attention:

> The faculty that is responsible more than any other for a person's coming to feel self-important and proud is wisdom. This is so because wisdom is a superior quality of the person himself, a function of his most honored faculty, intelligence. But there is no sage who will not err, and will not need to learn from the words of his friends and, very often, even from those of his pupils. How, then, can he pride himself in his wisdom? . . . As is stated by R. Yochanan ben Zakkai (*Avot* 2:9), "If you have learned much Torah do not take credit for it, for you were created to do so." One who is wealthy may rejoice in his lot, but at the same time he must help those in need. If one is strong, he must assist the weak and rescue the oppressed. (*Mesillat Yesharim*, 284)

For all his insight, there is no excoriation; nothing diminishes the Ramchal's respect for the created being. The author begins with generality and proceeds through human rather than logical reasoning to action, morally satisfying and rich in understanding. And we see clearly that he is often discussing very high levels of spiritual attainment, even for his own time. It did not fall to him to bear with open controversy and opposition on the principles of faith itself, as his successors in Jewish leadership have frequently had to do. The rabbinic authority was clearly recognized; his people were aware of imperatives and were strong enough to heed a rebuke:

> How many starve themselves and stoop to feeding from charity so as not to engage in an occupation they feel is lacking in respectability, for fear of a diminution of their honor? Is there anything sillier? They prefer to dwell in idleness, which leads to stagnation, lewdness and theft, and to all the major sins in order not to lower themselves and detract from the honor they imagine themselves to possess. . . . "Flay a carcass in the marketplace, and do not say, 'I am an important person; I am a priest.'" (*Pesachim* 113a) (*Mesillat Yesharim*, 170)

In those times, people were ready to be taught punishments as well as rewards, and the "yoke of heaven" was a familiar fact of life from early childhood. The whole picture presented by society was of a divine order, damaged by those who acted contrarily, but maintained by the well-taught paths on which honest people walked. Today, our concept of maintaining the world is almost entirely physical; the moral aspect no longer comes so readily to the hand. It is banished to the realm of metaphor; if a man were to "flay a carcass" in this way, no one would understand what he was doing. Yet in this remote realm, it still remains for us to understand, to assimilate into our consciousness to the extent that we are able. Though men of spiritual standing may be rare among us, we can still comprehend what it must have been to live among many of them. At the time of the Ramchal, there were such men in every community, and the high places where they dwelt were visible for all to see:

> The fear of sin that we are here concerned with is in one respect part of the awe of Divine Majesty mentioned above, and, in another, a distinct entity. It consists in a person constantly fearing and worrying that some trace of sin might have intruded itself into his actions, or that they contain something, small or great, that is inconsonant with the grandeur of the Blessed One's honor. . . . The fear of Divine Majesty obtains only during the performance of a deed . . . or upon the materialization of an opportunity for transgression. . . . The fear of sin, however, obtains at all periods and times. . . . In relation to this it is said (Proverbs 28:14), "Happy is the man who fears always," which our Sages of blessed memory interpreted (*Berachot* 60a) as referring to matters of Torah (*Mesillat Yesharim*, 312)

A generation that saw truths like these practiced before its eyes could not fail to know the difference between success and failure. They saw people whose strivings were not only directed to a proper goal but were recognizable as a union of strength with intention:

> The man whose soul burns in the service of his Creator will surely not idle in the performance of His *mitzvot*, but his

movements will be like the quick movements of a fire; he will not rest or be still until the deed has been completed. Furthermore, just as zeal can result from an inner burning, so it can create one. That is, one who perceives a quickening of his outer movements in the performance of a *mitzvah* conditions himself to experience a flaming inner movement, through which longing and desire will continually grow. If, however, he is sluggish in the movement of his limbs, the movement of his spirit will die down and be extinguished. (*Mesillat Yesharim*, 88)

More psychology, from behavior therapy to the anguish and loneliness of existentialism, is encompassed in these few comments than would fill many volumes of research today. Things once known to the wise must be forgotten in order to be rediscovered much later by ordinary people; it is as if the wise themselves mark out the ground for the developments that follow them. Their sight alone has an effect in actuality; nothing of their contribution is ever lost, though it flow into a million rivulets far from the source. Even at that extreme, their truth maintains its innate reality, irrigating the fields of thought and service, cultivating what is useful and disposing with what is unproductive. So it is with *The Path of the Just*; its existence is not merely that of a printed volume, even one with the power to mold and guide the lives of those who read it. It is in effect a path in itself, a path carved into the ways of heaven by its author so that its influence may be felt among us here below. Though it was written in a particular time, it was always above time, its true reality still abiding in the firmament from which it was culled.

TEACHER TO THE NEW WORLD

The book was published in Amsterdam in 1740, in both a "pocket book" edition and a more elaborate production embellished with poems and with ornamental engraving. Immediately, it achieved worldwide fame; nothing like it had ever been seen before, and no one was willing to pass up the chance to learn from it. The city itself became established as one of Jewry's "capitals of the spirit," beyond even the most optimistic hopes of the men who had made a place there available for the Ramchal. He continued his tasks, living quietly with his family out of the public eye while the last remnants of his opposition subsided into the past. Though he took no part in public affairs, he was still close to the community life as he had been in Padua, a companionable adviser and friend to the local families and to visitors from all over the world.

Once again he could write undisturbed, and in this period he seemed to have abandoned Kabbalah entirely, in favor of rabbinic subjects and especially methodology. Small, succinct "guides" to every detailed aspect of study and practice came steadily forth: *The Way of Understandings* to aid in learning Talmud and *The Discourse on Wisdom*, an introduction to the entire spectrum of knowledge, both human and divine. He developed to its peak the faculty he had begun to exercise in Italy for guiding the Jews through true paths according to the situations that confronted them.

As in Padua, he gathered around him a small

circle of close pupils, men of great reputation in their own right, with whom he discussed and set forth the concepts that marked out his thought. They in turn passed on his teachings to others, so that in the city there was a constant traffic of learning associated with him, among both visitors and residents. He taught very little Kabbalah, but his main work on the subject, *Gates of Wisdom* (*Kalach Pit'chei Chochmah*), which had been published in Padua, was consulted by those wishing to approach him from this direction.

Slowly but surely his circle was widening to embrace many aspects of life; indeed, a whole way of life was springing up in close association with his personality. Something of it still survives among Western Sephardim, and as he extended his benefit to their growing communities in colonial America, he became the earliest great Jewish influence on that country as a whole, as well as on the Jews themselves.

Great numbers of people in the United States today trace their religious foundations to this period, which followed the decline of the Quaker and Puritan regimes and saw the colonies reach the first threshold of selfhood and security. Their distinctively American approach to life and morality bears a strong resemblance to the Ramchal's way: kindness and hospitality within a facade of reserve, a consciousness of the importance of activity, ostensibly formal but really serving to express deep inner feeling, a fundamentalism appropriate to those who truly live among fundamentals. Thornton Wilder has spoken of how Americans are "abstract," oriented to everywhere and everything, the factor that makes for their relatively painless geographic and social mobility; this is the heritage of true belief, the ability to be rooted in divinity no matter what the outside conditions may bring.

This abstraction is the quality uppermost in the Ramchal's writings, as in the course of his whole life. He was able to bend like a supple reed, to be tossed and turned without ever falling: the adaptability of sainthood. The concepts of his time were those that formed the basis of American freedom, giving rise to the land that, after its slow maturation, came to be the haven for the bulk of world Jewry. Thus, it was on the Western shore of the Atlantic Ocean that his influence took root most firmly; the blend of simplicity and intelligence, the sweetness and trust came to make a core for the life of the New World.

Again he turned to the drama as a vehicle, writing a play for the wedding of one of his pupils to a daughter of the famous Henriques family, still prominent wherever the Sephardim of the Netherlands came to settle. *Migdal Oz* had been an idyll of people, but this play reached a further level of abstraction; it is an allegory whose characters bear the names of spiritual concepts. Their interplay is here also on a level of "innocence at large," of the struggle to maintain purity through the travails of the world, but the tone is more didactic, much less "youthful" and optimistic. *Praise to the Upright* (*Layesharim Tehillah*) is for those who come to see a serious play.

The allegory is if anything closer to our comprehension: Truth has a son, Upright, and People a daughter, Praise, and as the title shows, both parents agree that their children should marry when they come of age. At the same time Passion, who is enslaved to Truth, has a son, Proud, who lives with his mother in the house of Truth. One day the army of Confusion attacks the city, and both Upright and Proud are among the captives; after many years, Proud attempts to supplant Upright by marrying Praise.

However, Truth has already forestalled him by leaving his son's identity on record with the city magistrates; after the false wedding is wrecked by a thunderbolt, the real story emerges. Reason speaks on Upright's behalf; he then marries Praise in a joyous ceremony. Again the plot forms a "diagram of universality," a sketch of the modes of the heart as they succeed one another in the life of an individual. In Amsterdam, the Ramchal does not use the stage in its Italian manner, to transport his audience into a fantastic dimension; this is a journey into inner consciousness, where people are drawn closer to themselves. Among the Northern influences of light and shadow, we come closer than ever to the Ramchal's true introspection.

The play's dialogue, with its many additional characters and subplots, has a rich variety of shades of meaning, more than can be rendered properly into another language. The complexity has challenged lovers of Hebrew from the outset, not to mention the depth of Kabbalah understanding required to assimilate the author's intentions. Unlike *Migdal Oz*, the play immediately became well known, and it now joins the early work as the "grandfather" of storytelling for Jewish concepts. More sophisticated than the stories of R. Nachman of Breslov, they too allow a scholar to feel the enjoyment of a simple person and convey deep ideas to those otherwise not equipped to learn. A wedding reveler intently watches a play: every wedding that founds a Jewish family is a foundation of the Third Temple, and the Ramchal adds his knowledge at this juncture so that the building may truly be able to stand.

9

The Land of Israel

We have no record of how the Ramchal came to leave Amsterdam for the Land of Israel. From the perspective of history, it is as if he simply ceased to be in one place and appeared in another: not that it was in any way surprising for him to seek his life's consummation in the Holy Land. He was thirty-six years old, only four years distant from the turning point of forty, which had always been considered the minimum age for a man to bear the study of Kabbalah. Then he would be free from the restrictions imposed on him in Padua, able to continue in his chosen path without fear of reproach. Generations of *tzaddikim* before him had sought to do this on the holy soil, ever since Nachmanides (R. Moshe ben Nachman) had reestablished Jewish worship in Jerusalem in the thirteenth century after finding the site itself all but deserted, in a sense the deepest point of the exile. Since then, the Holy Land had become the final haven for all

115

those, great men and small, who sought only to perpetuate the way of the Torah in the place nearest to heaven, whence the Divine Providence was channeled to all the world.

Physically the country showed the results of the centuries of desolation and neglect. Food was extremely scarce; the wandering tribes tilled a small yield of crops from patches of bottomland that had escaped the depredations of goats and sheep. Dune and swampland encroached from the extremities, rendering the climate unhealthy. By this time, the Turkish regime was devoid of conscientiousness, snoring away its functions under a coverlet of *"baksheesh."* There were almost no visitors in the normal course of events, the country being considered "off the beaten track." But the spiritual serenity remained; Jews from all across the exile clung tenaciously to the sacred ground, studying and praying without distraction. They lived on money sent from communities abroad; the country was a favored place for charitable contributions, since the giver thereby purified all his material possessions, becoming merged in the "air of wisdom" found only there. It was a place fitted for the Jewish spirit; evil could not attain a complete conquest there, as it could in ordinary countries. The divine goodness was present in its pathways, visible in its providence for all who had eyes to see.

There was only one safe harbor along the coastline; Jaffa was a roadstead for boats to anchor offshore, but Acco in the north was an ancient city with a wharfside used for centuries in residual trade with Europe. The Crusaders had made it their main port of transit, building extensive harbor works and fortifications; in 1799 it was to be the scene of the country's tumultuous return to the center of world affairs as Napoleon's siege of the Turkish garrison succumbed to the arrival of the British fleet. At the time the Ramchal arrived, however, it was a sleepy fishing port, occasionally receiving a ship calling from farther afield. The *tzaddik* came with his wife and two young children and set up house in the town, traveling to the other communities and the holy sites, living a life of peaceful mutual acceptance with all around him. No controversy could follow him here; nothing could impair the reputation he had gained in Amsterdam.

It was a tranquil scene, but the tranquility was only apparent. He wrote briefly to David Franco Mendes and his other pupils in Amsterdam of his love for them, hinting at the exciting preoccupations of his new home:

This is a "sign" of love, a witness to how I have loved you in the inner workings of my heart, written with a pen of steel but fragrant like spice, of how I would convey my peace to you even from afar. Though I have but little time, for it is not given to me to write all the letters I need, but must wait until I have more leisure and my occupations decrease, I shall try to expand on this while I await a more favorable moment. In the goodness of your hearts, please accept this little in lieu of much, and may it be the peace of your portion and your happiness for length of days.

With the love of a pure heart,
Moshe Chaim Luzzatto (*Yarim Moshe*, רסנ)

This letter, at once greeting and farewell, is the last that we have from his hand. From here on is only silence, as if the occupations mentioned had taken up his time entirely. What was he doing there, so far from the centers of life and population? What made his studies different from what they had been in the countries of the exile?

WATERS OF RESTORATION

The Talmud states that the Land of Israel shrinks like a deerskin when the Jews are not living on it and expands when they return. We in our own time have witnessed an aspect of this complex and intriguing reality, where the growth of *Eretz Yisrael* in the world's estimation is among the dominant facts of international life, but even this is not truly what the rabbis of the Talmud meant. The *tzaddikim* who embarked on the journey to the Holy Land, whose every step in life was a step toward that goal, were engaged in a spiritual rebuilding, an expansion of consciousness in upper worlds of which our physical reality is only a reflection. There are certain commandments that can only be observed there; they constitute the very destiny of Creation itself, and only the man who truly desires to perform them will find within the borders of the physical land that haven of divinity described in the holy books. There are many barriers to achieving this, adversities that sometimes not even the strength of the righteous can overcome. Moses had yearned to go across the Jordan in order to fulfill these precepts, but was not permitted to do so; his latter-day namesake had achieved that end. Once in the Holy Land he became serene, free to advance without hindrance from level to level, returning to the center all that he had gathered on the periphery. He was still a writer, but writing had taken on a different value for him. There was no longer such a need to give instruction; his life itself would serve as an example. While there, he wrote no major book on either the revealed or esoteric aspect of Torah, but, as if in a burst of ecstasy, wrote one poem to form the culmination of his work in verse: the long "Hot Springs of Tiberias."

This lakeside town, one of the four holy cities of the Land, had always been known for its thermal waters, mentioned in Rashi's Torah commentary as among the "fountains of the deep" left open for this purpose after the subsiding of the Flood. It was called "king of waters," the greatest healing spa in the world, frequented by Roman emperors, Crusader dukes, Turkish emirs, and the rabbis of the Talmud themselves when their assembly was held in the town. The Ramchal chooses a startlingly free verse to depict the setting and the inner meaning of the springs, far distant from the conventions and restraints usual in the verse of the time. He describes the lake and mountain surroundings, graphically depicting the formation of the waters deep in the earth, and compares them to the Jewish people in exile who "flow underground" across the world, under sulfurous heat and tremendous pressures until they come to the surface in the Holy Land to find themselves endowed with curative powers. He sketches the mountainous scene with a liberal hand:

glimmers of frozen dew
crowning their heads, sceptered with stones of hail
like rainbow-view, confounding the objectors who would
    tread their hall;
a footstool bright with amethyst and agate.

The royal metaphor bears a resemblance to the usual pattern of the Ramchal's verse, but, on closer inspection, turns out to be deeply transformed. No longer does the author search for words to construct a scene out of a spiritual concept; here the scene is actual, already endowed with spiritual symbolism, needing only a quasiliteral description to convey its meaning. This "living metaphor" is the distinctive property of the Holy Land, the land of truth, made to exemplify elevated concepts, where the facts of life are those of morality and righteousness. We sense the Ramchal glorying in this scene, where the richest of vocabulary barely suffices to convey the depth and intensity of emotion. In details that must have been personally felt, he describes the soothing of the pains of exile in the warm spring water:

to channel the heart's pain away, to soothe abrasion,
take off the strain from belly, liver, kidney.
the grinding passes from the short of spirit, spot from
    off the flesh;
the hand of God has done this, worked this wonder.

The spring itself is a symbol of the entire Land, a spiritual "healing spa," filled with waters to revive the soul; the actual waters are a physical example of the curative power, of an entirely new way of life. The author compares the tribulations of the Jews with the subterranean processes at work to form the waters:

> these are salvation's fountains, sundered from their place
> on nethermost floors, great wanderings through stone and
>   iron.
> behold their strength, the waters rubbed with sulfur and
>   with lead;
> their taste and smell reversed there, turned to healing power.

The form and meter achieve a freedom and vitality almost unprecedented in that era, worlds apart from the obvious constrictions of the "exilic" forms employed in Italy. This boundlessness has an import of its own, recalling the words of King Solomon in the "Song of Songs": "The voice of my Beloved! here He comes, leaping over the mountains, skipping across the hills . . ." (Song of Songs 2:9). It is the world of the liberated spirit, of the revelation of the Holy Name, the world of the restored House of God.

When the Ramchal entered the Holy Land, he brought with him the temple of himself, restoring it to its proper place, with consequences beyond even our own time, both within and outside the country. Other *tzaddikim* also made the journey, such as R. Nachman of Breslov (who was in Acco during the French siege) and the previous Lubavitcher Rebbe. They too brought their own achievements to a consummation, acquiring a divine confidence and ease of understanding quite evident in their demeanor. Rabbi Nachman would even say that he had known nothing before he came to the Land, and that his arrival was the only merit he could honestly claim. Both of these men subsequently returned to Europe, taking their knowledge of the country out into their subsequent lives, but for the Ramchal, the consummation was to be a final one.

In those times of brokenness, disease was an ever-present threat; in May of 1746, when the hot weather began, the town was swept by an outbreak of cholera, and the *tzaddik* and his family were among those taken away. It was the 26th of *Iyar*, the date equal to the numerical value of the Divine Name, and whose *sefirah* in the counting of the *Omer* is "Foundation of Foundation." Europe heard the news from a proclamation circulated by the rabbis of Tiberias:

> Hear, O heavens, and give ear, O earth, how the great among rabbis, the divine kabbalist, the Lamp, Chariot of Israel and his horsemen, the light that was in Israel, our teacher and master R. Moshe Chaim Luzzatto, has passed away, he and all his family, of the pestilence before the Lord. He has been interred in Tiberias next to Rabbi Akiva, peace be upon him. Happy is his lot, in this world and in the World to Come, but woe is to us, for the Crown has fallen from our heads.

He was thirty-nine years old, the acknowledged prime mover of Jewry in his day, victor over all his opponents, against whom no one could any longer say a word. His tomb stands on a hillside overlooking the Sea of Galilee, in a setting that many have compared with the Italy of his birth: lake and mountain beauty, a warm wind rustling through the olive trees. As the funeral procession wound its way back to the town, the Jewish world was left to ponder and come to terms with the

meaning and impact of his contribution. Generations were to pass before this task could even
begin, and by then his works were also underground, hidden by the dust of later emergencies
and struggles. The Baal Shem Tov later said that
the Ramchal had been the manifestation of Mashiach ben Yosef, the mystical principle of kingship
originating in Joseph himself, which is subsumed
in the eventual redemptive reality. It was also said
that he had been a reincarnation of the soul of
Maimonides, his only superior as a writer on Jewish thought, come to complete the designated
task.

INHERITANCE

True to the principle that after death the righteous
are present in the world more than in their lifetime, even in this physical world itself, his influence grew until it became all pervading. Those
who had been near him in Padua and Amsterdam
spread out all across Europe with their knowledge
and their personal memories of the man. Yekutiel
Gordon, in particular, took on the task of disseminating his teacher's ideas as widely as possible.
Apart from this, however, the memories were few;
the Ramchal had lived in countries with small Jewish populations, so he never became the focus of
adoration by great numbers, like Maimonides, or
a source for folktales as did the leaders of the North.
Only through his works and the impression of his
epoch-making struggles would he pass into the col-
lective consciousness; thus, for subsequent times

his reputation was largely confined to the educated minority. The bulk of the observant people thought of him as a kind of luminous presence in the upper spiritual firmament, a being essentially beyond the usual range of contacts.

When his successors took up the threads, it was on a very different basis, owing to the complex changes that the situation had undergone. Within only a few years, the Baal Shem Tov in Poland inaugurated the chasidic movement, the revelation of new forms of understanding derived from Kabbalah, which marked the decisive change from the methods and customs of the past. His successor was Rabbi Dov Baer of Miezrich, known as the *Maggid*, who was once asked by a learner why the Ramchal had passed away so young. He replied that the generation of those days had not been worthy of the Ramchal's level, an answer that hinted at the conditions under which he himself was working. Before he taught his *Chasidut* in public, the *Maggid* would study the Ramchal's *Kalach Pit'chei Chochmah* (*138 Gates of Wisdom*) in order to find the orientation that his predecessor's work had provided in the universe. The *chasidim* were not following directly on the Ramchal's path, but rather established their way as a consequence of the "earthquake" he had wrought in the existing conditions. They rarely quoted him openly, out of awe for the heights he had reached immediately prior to their time. His name would have been so powerful to them that they could not avail themselves of it. He was the "secret friend," the man who showed the path to safety and just as quickly returned to his mysterious abode. For it was his influence on the *mitnagdim*, those who opposed the chasidic movement, that would hold them on a firm level of religious life, a direct consequence of his victory over his own attackers.

The *mitnagdim* studied his ethical works in great detail, basing their entire way of life on his homiletical principles. For over two hundred years, they retained their close attachment to outward aspects of his contribution, though their leaders remained in touch with the Kabbalah depths as well. Greatest among them was the Gaon of Vilna, who said that if he had been alive in the Ramchal's time, he would have traveled to Italy on foot all the way from the Baltic in order to learn from him; this was the feeling uppermost in the hearts of his followers through the succeeding generations. Like the *Maggid*, he was passing on the Ramchal's teachings in an unspoken form, though it was he who made use of the works themselves, but the difference lay in the fact that on this basis the *chasidim* were making advances in their own right, while their opponents remained on the level that the Ramchal had established for them. The streams flowed apart, branching again many times within both of the main distributaries, until they came within reach of a recognition of the unity that had preceded them.

All the while the Ramchal's teachings were being passed down the line of chasidic leaders, from master to pupil, in something close to their entirety, an inseparable part of leadership and guidance in general. Rabbi Shneur Zalman, the first Lubavitcher Rebbe, who had been born the year before the Ramchal's passing, had wrought a fundamental change in the whole course of Jewish life when he traveled to Miezrich to learn from the *Maggid*, and his teacher gave him the wisdom he had found in the searches he made before he would begin to impart to others. Thus was formed the basis of the modern Jewish world, the element that would sustain it through dispersion and war and the undermining of the practice itself. Was it the secrets of Kabbalah? Was it poetry, the foundation of chasidic song, the holiness of melody and joy? Or ethical guidance, the calm, confident voice of the man versed in the pitfalls of life? There was always a riddle at the heart of the matter, to counterpoise the logical, deductive faculty that seemed so much to the fore. But this was the way of one separated from mundane contingencies, of a man who lived through the divine dimension; this was the way of a king.

A king . . . when the kingship of the House of David was restored, everything would come to fruition. The revelation of the Divine Name among mankind would put an end to the life of correction and trial. Torah would be restored to its former glory, and knowledge "poured out" on all the nations. In every generation the true leader knows how his people stand in relation to this; the Ramchal had judged it necessary in his time to cull from the sources everything that described this change and the processes leading to it. He presented it in the form of an orderly *Discourse on Redemption* (*Maamar ha-Geulah*), adopting an almost conversational mode of address, giving over the majestic concepts as if he were talking with a friend. Never before had such a deep analysis been compiled for everyone to read, never had the Kabbalah secrets involved been laid before the public:

> You must know that there are two distinct periods within the Redemption itself, one relating to the Egyptian release and one to the Babylonian. These are alluded to in the quotation I mentioned at the outset (Micah 7:8): "Rejoice not against me, O mine enemy; though I am fallen, I shall arise," this being the first period. . . . "Though I sit in darkness, the Lord is a light to me," this being the second. The hint is found not only in this place but in others also. . . . I shall undertake to explain these periods to you, with the very deep secrets that they involve, but since they are so deep I shall not discuss them at length but explain only what is intrinsic to an understanding. Bear this in mind and comprehend. . . . [During the "Egyptian" period] when the power appointed for remedy stemming from the perfect root of things is conferred upon the *tzaddik*, who is termed in the Torah "Angel of Redemption," then this great luminary will descend and the *Shechinah* [Divine Presence] be revealed, being the "daughter of the Supernal Union," and She will possess powers not given her from the day of Israel's exile until that time. Then will be assembled such an assembly as will not have been seen since the day I mentioned until then. . . . When this is occurring, there will be no place for light altogether, such will be the gathering of darkness in those times. Israel will abandon hope of redemption, from their constriction of spirit and the onerous burdens upon them. This is the meaning of the question in the Song of Songs (5:2): "I have taken off my garments [to sleep]; how can I put them on again?" the "garments" being those of Understanding.

Ours is an age when light of the kind given to earlier generations is indeed almost unknown. Most of world Jewry has forgotten what it is to understand the ways of the Creator. Our eyes are so used to the darkness that we fear the light even more; our gropings have become second nature, and the life of the city seems the only reality given to man. When the Ramchal looked into the Torah, he saw the future. Destiny lay before him to do with as he thought best, and he saw to it that when these times arrived people would be comforted in the knowledge that one before had written of how things would be. For so it is with the wise; a word in the right place, at the right time.

10

Excerpts from the Works of Ramchal

INTRODUCTION

The works of the Ramchal are very consistent in style, and the following excerpts have been chosen to illustrate as many of his individual processes as possible. It is another remarkable facet of his approach that such a selection serves to illustrate the range of key points in the subject matter as well. The almost Germanic thoroughness and assurance are a protective shield for a form of humor, which, though also Germanic in superficial aspect, has a much lighter touch, and when seen more closely proves to be extremely subtle and far reaching. This is the "mystery of existence" so well known in all Jewish humor, and in the Ramchal's highly intellectualized formulation, it has a place so close to the heart of the matter as to be worth investigation in its own right.

The *Derech Tevunot* (*Ways of Reason*) on talmudic logic has in chapter 10 on "Order of Study," a brief scheme of the talmudic logical structure as a whole. The *Gemara* itself develops through four stages, summarized here as follows:

- the statement itself in all its parts
- understanding the purpose behind the making of this statement
- examining how the statement serves this purpose
- verification of this examining process in all its stages.

These four stages correspond respectively to the four letters of the Divine Name, "*Yud*," "*Heh*," "*Vav*," "*Heh*," representing the initial divine wisdom, the higher understanding, the emotional attributes that select and develop the higher mentalities, and the lower or practical understanding. The Ramchal does not explain this correspondence directly here, though in other extracts quoted he does so; his intention is to render the *Gemara* itself easily intelligible to the learner in this way, through the highest form of simple practicality.

FROM *DAAT TEVUNOT*

INTELLECT: The essence of man proceeds from profound, unfathomable wisdom. The Creator fashioned many great creations, each greater than the last, and others still greater above them. All of them are indispensable, since nothing is created in vain, but all of them stand on a single foundation, namely, that goal which the Blessed One desires man to accomplish through his service; to correct all the imperfections in the creation and to raise himself in ascent after ascent until he unites himself with the Blessed One's holiness. To this end, He invested the universe with all those agencies which foster removal from Him, with all of their ramifications, and also with all those which foster alliance with Him, with all of their ramifications. These are all awesomely profound, and all are so attuned as to resolve themselves into the universal perfection.

And the Supreme Will desired that man be involved in all of them, so that they might all be moved by his movements and actions. They can be compared, as it were, to a great mechanism, a kind of clock, whose wheels are conjoined in such a way that one small wheel moves many larger ones. Thus has the Blessed One conjoined all of His creations in great ties, and connected everything to man, so that he through his deeds is the mover and all the others are moved by him. And He has concealed all of this behind the earthy covering of skin and flesh, so that only this bodily layer is visible. But in truth there are great things behind it, great mechanisms that the Holy One, blessed be He, created in His world in concourse with the deeds and divine service of man; toward his ascent and growth in holiness, or (God forbid) his descent and falling off in it, and all of the many other states.

However, this concerns only the godly soul (*neshamah*), which He included in the body of man in all of its roots and divisions. This is what King

David referred to when he said (Psalm 40:6), "You have done many things, O Lord my God, Your wonders and Your thoughts toward us," and (134:14) "I will thank You, for I have been singled out for wonders. Your deeds are wondrous, and my soul knows it well." For the body cannot conceive of these things as can the soul, since they are evident not through earthiness but only through spirituality.

One of the aspects of this mechanism, as we have explained, is evil in all of its facets, with all the other necessities of man in the situation of this world. And all of these serve the end of the revelation of God's Oneness, the revelation of light from within darkness. From the initial concealment of His countenance in all of its ramifications will follow the revelation of Oneness in the end. Now we must understand that the Supreme Will desired the active manifestation of the truth of His Oneness, by means of all the cycles that He sets in motion in His universe, as we see from the verse (Isaiah 43:10) "So that you should know and believe Me, and understand that I am God." and similarly (Deuteronomy 32:39), "See now that I, I am He."

For in the beginning He desires to manifest this in actuality, and therefore sets the entire cycle in motion to resolve itself in favor of this point. And accordingly when this has been achieved and manifested, from then on will ensue unification and attainment, as His creatures reach union with Him and rejoice in the perfection of His Oneness now that it is revealed. They will bask in the splendor of His presence, and attain through this perfection states more profound than the first, without end, through all eternity.

We find, therefore, two varieties of action in respect to the Blessed One. The first is what He will do after His Oneness is revealed and actively believed in by human beings. This embraces the generality of reward and recompense, whose essence and details cannot now be apprehended by the body. What we know for certain, however, is that the general character of this reward can be described as "basking in the splendor of the Blessed One's holiness," as our Sages have stated, (*Berachot* 17a) "The righteous sit with their crowns on their heads and bask in the splendor of the *Shechinah*."

And unquestionably there will be many different varieties of pleasure, by implication from what we see in this world, which is like a fleeting shadow and yet has had many different varieties of pleasure invested in it by the Creator for humanity to enjoy, although they are in general pleasures for the senses alone. How much more should this be so in the world that is entirely good? Although the pleasures there will be of one kind only, namely, the spiritual good of understanding and of union with God, still the facets of that good will be of great diversity. This is the meaning of what I stated concerning the providence of the Blessed One: that it was originated only to give rise to spiritual states of holiness.

The second variety of action is what the Blessed One does while this truth is revealing itself and its process of revelation is still incomplete. This time lasts from the beginning of creation to the ultimate redemption (may it come speedily and in our days), it having been said of that time (Zechariah 14:9), "And God will be King over all the earth. On that day the Lord will be One and His Name One."

All of the mechanisms that we mentioned above relate to this second variety, the revelation of God's Oneness through the concealment of countenance which precedes it. And involved in these mechanisms is the idea of evil that we discussed. Thus, while evil in itself is nothing but defect, loss, and destruction, still, in conjunction with the other mechanisms, it is the source of man's good itself. For upon it hinges all of merit and all possibility of divine service, this by its being intended not to conquer but to be conquered. It exists only to be hewn down by man, like the stone at the crossroads in the aforementioned parable.

Evil was created in order to be destroyed, and thus it may be regarded in two ways, either in point of its existence or in point of its eradication, its beginning or its end. In terms of its beginning, it is certainly evil, but its end is all to the good, for at the very time it is asserting its power it is acting as the precursor of good. This is the darkness through which the light of the Supreme perfection will be recognized when it reveals itself in time to come. What is more, this is the elucidation of the truth of His Oneness in all of its vividness, as we explained above. The darker it grows, the greater will be the revelation of the truth of His Oneness when He destroys this evil. Further still, the evil offers a gain to the one who is tested by it, as in the parable of our Sages concerning the prostitute sent by the king to test the prince (*Berachot*

32a). It creates for man the opportunity for true service and action, for with his own hands he perfects the creation and removes its defects, becoming as it were a partner in the world with the Holy One, blessed be He.

FROM *DERECH HASHEM*:
"THE ORDER OF THE DAY"

In order to understand the significance of the *Amidah* we must first be aware of a number of fundamental concepts.

God's influences in general are related to all Creation through the Tetragrammaton, the four-lettered ineffable Name, "*Yud*" "*Heh*" "*Vav*" "*Heh*." The highest influences are divided into three major categories, and these include all types of influence and their details. These three categories are alluded to by the first three letters of the Tetragrammaton. In order for all Creation to be perfected, these three letters must be brought together, and their interconnection is alluded to by the final letter "*Heh*."

These three primary categories are also alluded to in the initial descriptions of God found in the *Amidah*, namely, "*Gadol, Gibbor*, and *Nora*."

The concept that properly transmits these three categories is the merit of the three Patriarchs, Abraham, Isaac, and Jacob. This in turn is completed by the merit of King David, which brings them all together, and thus he is associated with the Patriarchs in completing the rectification of Israel.

The first three blessings of the *Amidah* were

ordained to parallel these three categories, and through these blessings, the highest sustenance is transmitted generally. The thirteen middle blessings then transmit the details of this sustenance as it is needed. Finally, through the three final blessings, this sustenance is strengthened and integrated in its recipients through the thanks that are given for it. This is the significance of the *Amidah* in general.

This is the weekday order, but on holy days only seven blessings were ordained. These days have their own intrinsic blessing and sanctity, which transmit God's sustenance, and therefore only a general effort is needed, consisting of the seven blessings. The first and last three are the same as for the weekdays, and the middle blessing relates to the general sanctity of the day, causing it to be strengthened, shine forth, and rule, thus enhancing and perfecting every detail of Creation.

It is also necessary to realize that there are four general universes. The first is the physical, divided into the astronomical and the terrestrial, namely, the stars and planets and the Earth on which we live. Above this is another universe, the world of angels. Higher than this is still another universe, which is the domain of the highest forces (*kochot*) and is known as the Universe of the Throne. Higher still we may speak of God's influences in general, consisting of revelations of His Light, from which all existence is derived and upon which it all depends. In figurative terms these influences in general can be said to constitute a universe, and therefore it is referred to as the Universe of Godliness (*Elokut*), but properly speaking only the three lower domains can be called by this term. The reason for this is that a universe is defined as a collection of many diverse entities and principles, divided and interrelated in various ways in a single conceptual space, whether its entities are physical or spiritual. God's influences, however, cannot be considered plural or diverse beings in any way whatsoever. Rather, they are all distinctions and revelations of God's Light, differentiated only by the fact that He avails Himself of them for the benefit of the various things that He created. These recipients are the roots of all divisions, orders, and sequences, as we have explained.

These universes depend upon and result from those which stand above them, in the order in which they are given here, the physical upon the angels, and so on. The four portions of the daily service also follow this order; the sacrificial readings (*Korbanot*) pertain to the physical world, the praises (*Pesukei d'Zimrah*) to the angels, the Shema and its blessings to the Universe of the Throne (being essentially concerned with the acknowledgment of the divine rulership), and the Amidah to the Universe of Godliness, transmitting its influences according to their various aspects. The prayers and readings that follow (*U'Va le-tziyon, Shir shel Yom, En k'Elokenu,* and *Alenu*) likewise transmit a continuity of sustenance to the three worlds and conclude with a general establishment of sovereignty.

The entire day is also divided into four portions: the morning and afternoon, and the two equal parts of the night. Each of these requires an appropriate transmission of godly illumination in all of the universes for the true concept of the particular time of day.

It is for this reason that a fixed number of daily services was ordained. Since the morning is the time when God's sustenance is required for the day as a whole, it has a longer and more inclusive service of prayer (*Shacharit*). In the afternoon, on the other hand, only the latter part of the day must be perfected, and therefore a lesser amount of effort is required. Accordingly the afternoon service (*Minchah*) is the shortest of all. The difference between night and day is greater than that between morning and afternoon, and therefore nightfall involves a greater conceptual change. Thus the evening service (*Maariv*) is longer than that of the afternoon. It also contains the Shema and its blessings, but since the sustenance of the morning service is still retained, the blessings are much shorter.

No universal service was ordained for the latter part of the night, since this would overburden the community. However, a midnight service (*Tikkun Chatzot*) does exist, designated for the especially devout, who rise and cry out to God, each according to his own understanding.

FROM *MESILLAT YESHARIM*: "CONCERNING THE MEANS OF ACQUIRING SAINTLINESS"

The instrumental element in the acquisition of saintliness is much observation and thought. For when a person expends much thought on the greatness of the Blessed One's majesty, on His absolute perfection, and on the infinitely great gap between His sublimity and our lowliness, he will be filled with fear and tremble before Him. And through such dwelling upon His loving-kindness to us, upon the strength of the Blessed One's love for mankind, upon the nearness of the just to Him and upon the nobility of Torah and *mitzvot*, he will certainly likewise be fired with a strong love for God and will choose and lust to be united with Him.

For when he sees that the Blessed One is in fact a Father to us and pities us as a father pities his sons, he will naturally be awakened with a desire and a longing to reciprocate to Him, as a son to his father. But to acquire this attitude he must closet himself, and gather all of his knowledge and thought for consideration and study of the truths here mentioned. He will certainly be aided in this by much preoccupation with and close application to the *Tehillim* (Psalms) of King David (may peace be upon him), and by reflection upon their statements and ideas. For since the *Tehillim* are all filled with the love and fear of God and with all types of saintliness, in thinking upon them he cannot but be greatly inspired to follow in their author's footsteps and to walk in his ways. Also helpful is reading of those works telling of incidents in the lives of the pious, for they stimulate the intelligence to take counsel and to emulate these estimable deeds.

The deterrents to saintliness are preoccupation and worries. When one's intelligence is preoccupied and pressed with his worries and affairs, it cannot turn to the thoughts we speak of; and without such reflection saintliness cannot be attained. And even if one has already attained it, preoccupations continue to exert pressure on his mind and confuse it, not permitting him to strengthen himself in fear and love and in the other aforementioned aspects of saintliness. This is the intention behind the statement of our Sages of blessed memory (*Shabbat* 30b), "The *Shechinah* does not reside among sadness."

What we have said holds true also of enjoyments and pleasures; they are diametrically opposed to saintliness, because they induce the heart to be pulled along after them and to depart from all aspects of separation (*prishut*) and true knowledge.

However, a man can be protected against these deterrents and rescued from them by trusting to God, by casting his lot with Him in the realization that a person can never be deprived of what is set aside for him, as our Sages of blessed memory have said (*Beitzah* 16a), "A man's entire sustenance is determined for him on Rosh Hashanah," and (*Yoma* 38b) "A man cannot touch even a hairbreadth of what has been set aside for his neighbor."

A man could sit idle and what was thus ordained for him would materialize, were it not for the penalty imposed on all men (Genesis 3:19), "With the sweat of your brow shall you eat bread." Because of this divine decree, a man is required to exert himself somewhat for his sustenance. This is a tax, as it were, which must be paid by every member of the human race and which cannot be evaded. In the words of our Sages of blessed memory (*Sifrei*), "I would think that a man would be permitted to sit idle, had we not been told

[Deuteronomy 28:20], 'With all the putting forth of your hand which you undertake.'"

This is not to say that the exertion produces the results, but only that it is necessary. Once one has exerted himself, however, he has fulfilled his responsibilities and made room for the blessing of heaven to rest upon him, and he need not consume his days in striving and exertion. As King David (may peace be upon him) said (Psalm 75: 7, 8), "For not from east or west and not from the wilderness comes uplifting. This one He puts down, and this one He lifts up, for God rules." And King Solomon (may peace be upon him) said (Proverbs 23:4), "Do not weary yourself to become rich; cease from your understanding."

The correct approach in this matter is that of the early saints, who made their Torah primary and their labor secondary, and were successful in both. For once a man does a little work, he need only trust in his Master and not be troubled by any worldly concerns. His mind will then be free, and his heart ready for true saintliness and pure divine service.

FROM *DERECH TEVUNOT*: AUTHOR'S INTRODUCTION ON TALMUDIC STUDY

The pleasure in discovering truth is a natural trait of the intelligent soul that exists in every one of us. Any normal person, therefore, will make the utmost effort to reveal the true nature of anything he observes and banish falsehood.

If truth were self-evident, we could gain wisdom by simple observation. The more we observed the world around us, the wiser we would be. But in fact, whether we consider the observer or what he observes, this is not true. For all objects must be considered in terms of many different logical aspects, both intrinsic and relational, all of which are equally true. For example, the *shape* of a table and its measurements, *length*, *width*, and so forth, are intrinsic aspects of a table. The *use*, *worth*, and *age* are relational aspects.

To complicate matters even further, not all aspects are equally apparent. Some are readily observable through our senses, others less so, requiring great effort to discern them. The problem is compounded in the objects themselves, because the same aspect that is apparent in one object may be hidden in another. For example, the *use* of a table is readily apparent, namely, that food and utensils are placed on it; similarly, the *use* of bread is that it sustains mankind. However, the *use* of many wild plants can only be known, if at all, after long and intensive investigation. Thus we see that there is no object so apparent in all its aspects that its true nature can be understood solely through superficial observation.

Aside from these difficulties, experience shows us that many people imagine false ideas to be absolutely true. They generally remain firm in their beliefs, refusing to see anything wrong with them. After initial study, a person may think that his ideas are clear and true, and only afterward does he find them false and have to retract them. We can therefore say with certainty that the true nature of things is neither apparent nor readily understood, and there is in fact considerable room for mistakes, for what is false may appear true, and the human mind is not always discriminating enough to hit upon the truth. The mind may in fact even turn aside from the path of truth without being aware of doing so.

In the light of this, it is beneficial for a person to find guidelines and a method to keep himself on the straight path without straying. For if he does carelessly go astray, he will, after thorough observation, be able to recognize his error and return to the path. The basis of this method is the systematic compilation of all logical categories of things, explaining their functions and rules as they really are. This method is a guide, leading the mind unfalteringly in the search for wisdom. This is what our Sages of blessed memory meant when they praised King Solomon for making "handles for the Torah" (*Eruvin* 21b). He was able to acquire a large measure of knowledge with ease through the application of short, concise, and properly ordered rules. Now do not think that these rules are so profound that they are beyond the grasp of ordinary people. On the contrary, they are extremely simple and obvious. My sole innovation in this book is the step of conscious awareness and organization. Even though all these rules are really natural laws of thinking, they cannot help anyone unless they are consciously used and organized as a tool. Once they are so organized, a person has the "handles" with which to grasp the most profound and intricate ideas, as I have explained.

When I became aware of the great benefit and necessity of this study, I was moved to compose this small work. Anyone wishing to approach it seriously will enhance his own learning, and also his teaching of others. However, he must not minimize the task, for the way of the uneducated is to view everything simplistically. Read my words carefully and master every concept, for I have not been lax in choosing my words with exactness in order to express each point in the clearest possible way. My intention has been to arrange and explain the methods of understanding and knowledge in a style that is brief, yet sufficient. The goal of this method is to recognize truth and embrace it, and to uncover falsehood and reject it.

The Talmud is like a vast ocean set before us, whose arguments are mighty waves, whose laws roll forth rising to the heavens and plunging to the depths. Through the forward movement of these strong currents, the Truth of Torah is classified and distilled; this is called the Holy Way. It is in the Talmud that I have chosen to base my building, so that my method will be successful and immutable. This Torah method, then, is the paradigm for all understanding and wisdom.

I shall explain in detail the foundations of analytical argument in the Talmud, and the principles of its dialectic thought. This will help anyone who is not already familiar with Talmud study and desires to embark on it directly and easily. If he begins his study with the aid of this little book, he will find the avenues of talmudic law open to him, and he will travel along them without needless detour. What might have taken long hours, great concentration, and hard labor to acquire can be achieved with a minimum of time and effort, for he will be tremendously aided by an organized method and classification of ideas. Even someone who is already accustomed to Torah study may occasionally be kept from falling into error.

For this reason I have named the book *Derech Tevunot* in accordance with its main idea.

May the Almighty, who is the source of all knowledge and understanding, grant us knowledge, wisdom, and understanding, so that we may fear Him, do His will, and serve Him with a complete heart for all eternity. Amen, may such be His will.

FROM *DERECH TEVUNOT*: "ELEMENTS OF DEBATE"

Every talmudic discussion is built from seven principal elements of dialectic reasoning. They are: Statement, Question, Answer, Contradiction, Proof, Difficulty, and Resolution.

- Statement—the speaker states a single idea.
- Question—a person asks another a point of information.
- Answer—the person asked responds to the question.
- Contradiction—the speaker disproves a statement and totally refutes it.

- Proof—the speaker presents evidence from which the truth of statement or idea is made apparent.
- Difficulty—a person points out something untrue or unpleasing in a statement or idea.
- Resolution—a person turns aside the difficulty raised against a statement or idea.

Each of these statements has subcategories which will be explained later with the help of the Almighty.

It must be noted that dialectics are founded on first principles which are naturally found in our mind and which lead us to an understanding of any statement, and to an acceptance or rejection of ideas. Every difficulty and resolution, every proof and disproof and all the other parts of argumentation mentioned above are built on these foundations. . . .

There are three processes that the mind uses in pursuit of understanding:

The first is the building of a complete picture of the subject and an exact understanding of statements and ideas as they are intended.

The second is the derivation of new ideas from a stated premise.

The third is the acceptance or rejection of each premise and conclusion on the basis of proof.

In each of these processes the mind proceeds according to natural principles as we mentioned, and as we shall see further with the help of the Almighty. Now we shall explain each process individually in detail.

FROM *MAAMARIM*

PRAYER FOR ROSH HASHANAH

We have already explained how on this holy day the Holy One, blessed be He, stands in the manner of King over His world, and thus it is for us to gain strength from this, since it is all of our good and our capacity. Furthermore, this is a day of trial and judgment, and we are required to reveal ourselves before Him (may he be blessed), to elevate our merits before Him for good.

And there is another important concept on this day, namely, the *"shofar"* in which we are commanded, since its blowing here on earth and its root above is the special concept which strengthens the good and denies the evil. After the sin of *Adam ha-Rishon*, the good was intermingled with the evil and repressed under it, but it emerged from its imprisonment to be reestablished in its own right, leaving the evil separate and distinct once more. In the future era this restoration will be completed altogether, and the good will conquer the evil entirely, ruling once more in supremacy, but the prime mover toward this end was the *shofar* heard at the Giving of the Torah, as it is written (Exodus 19:19), "The voice of the *shofar* continuing and strengthening."

Thus also the future restoration, when the good will achieve complete victory, will come through the *shofar*, as is written (Isaiah 17:13), "The great *shofar* will sound," and because this restoration will be complete, as no other which has ever been, it is called the "great" *shofar*. Accordingly we are commanded to sound the *shofar* on Rosh Hashanah, to strengthen the restoration which occurred at the Giving of the Torah, and to invite the anticipated completion. In this way also we arrange the order of the prayers for the day, to awaken this concept appropriately. Thus there are three general headings of concepts in the *Musaf* prayer to accomplish this task, namely *Malchiyot*, *Zichronot*, and *Shofarot*, and ten quotations within each of them, corresponding to the Ten Sayings of Creation, which represent the ten *sefirot*.

The "Sprinklings" in the Temple Service for Yom Kippur

The concept of the order of sprinklings of sacrificial blood, numbered as "One," "One and One," and so on, is as follows: that the result of our sins is a darkening of the Light in the seven lower *Sefirot*, and that in consequence there occurs—*chas ve-chalila*—a strengthening of the exterior forces according to the extent of the darkening. Therefore the *tikkun* ("restoration") for this is that light of understanding (*Binah*) should again shine in the seven lower *Sefirot*, strengthening and reinvigorating them, and in this way the exterior forces are humbled and broken.

Thus the first sprinkling serves to illuminate the *Sefirah* of *Binah* itself, and it is numbered solely as "One." The remaining sprinklings, each of one sprinkling above and one below, serve to arouse each of the seven lower *Sefirot* and to convey to it the illumination of understanding. Hence "One and One," One and Two," and so on, namely, One above for *Binah* and One below for *Chesed*, One for *Binah* and Two for *Gevurah*, and so on through all the Lower Seven entirely.

FROM *THE PARTICULARS OF GOVERNANCE*

And see how the foundation of this ordering is the order of "inwardness and outwardness," namely, the roots of the soul and the body respectively. Concerning this it is said, "I have made man in My image, according to My likeness," and thus this order is decreed from the very outset. Subsequently the order was divided into many luminaries, and the secret of this matter is the attributes of "kindness" and "judgment," since these are the prerequisites for reward and punishment. "Kindness" operates in "inwardness," and "judgment" in "outwardness"; this in general is how the Infinite One contracted His Light, and how it became a discernible operating factor. "Kindness" and "judgment" themselves resolve into "right" and "left" respectively, the attributes of "face" and "rear," and of "male" and "female." These are all different ways in which action occurs, but the secret common to them all is "kindness and judgment," divided into their different forms of action according to the needs of governance. From this power emanates man in his place, and it is necessary that these actions be arranged according to levels that relate to all of his bodily parts. Thus at first there was strength, and subsequently weakening, until our present situation was reached, and from this weakening proceeded many branches, each less than its predecessor, until the whole of the Creation stood complete; and the heart of it all is man.

FROM *TEFILLOT*

It is evident that no matter can be established more firmly than אמת, since it is the secret of Your unity, which never changes, as it is written, "I am Hashem; I have not changed." Therefore there is one who constantly guards אמת, namely, the letters "*Alef*," "*Mem*," "*Taf*" (the first, middle, and last letters of the "*Alef-Bet*") according to "beginning within end" of the verse "I am the beginning, I am the end, and beside Me there is no other," and also, "*Hashem* is near to all who call upon Him, to those who call upon Him in אמת."

Master of all worlds, in the truth of Your unity we call upon You, and even if all the adversaries in the world were to oppose us we would not abandon it. Rather, the "one who constantly guards truth" will push them aside. In the truth of Your unity we place our trust, fulfill before You, and pray to You; do not send us away from You empty-handed, for we hope in Your salvation, O Lord.

FROM *SEFER HIGAYON*: INTRODUCTION

When one contemplates the creations of the earth, and the events taking place among them, it is evident that the Almighty has given mankind a great part to play, in the settlement of this world and the destinies of all that is in it. It can be fairly said that in this respect the Creation itself was no more than a beginning, for all creatures and for their capacity of completion. In terms of action this capacity is entirely entrusted to mankind, and our Sages, be their memory for a blessing, have already awakened us to this truth in their statement that everything which was formed at the Creation stood in need of improvement: wheat must be ground, bitter legumes must be sweetened, and so forth. We find also that Turnus Rufus asked Rabbi Akiva, "Which works are more pleasing, those of heaven or those of man?" and was answered, "Those of man." In proof of his words, Rabbi Akiva brought sheaves of corn and baked cakes, and asked, "Which of these are more pleasing?"

And in truth we see with our own eyes that those products of nature that are left without human attention will continue to do as their nature ordains for them, but will not improve, and that when human efforts are expended upon them in such a way as to aid their nature, then their yield will be given in an orderly and pleasing manner. They will be seen to become more complete and fulfilled even in themselves, as is indeed well known. When a tree is left to itself, without attention, even though it will continue to give the fruit of its kind, that fruit will still not have the taste of fruit that has been brought into cultivation. Land which has not been cultivated will not easily be sown or grazed; either it will give no yield at all, or its products will be harsh and inferior. There are indeed localities where nature is very bountiful and there is almost no need for toil, but in general this is certainly not the case.

The general position is that the Creator made a place for mankind, appropriate to the capacity of their hands. where by their labors they would cultivate and gather what nature itself provides; and thus also concerning the human intellect, that a state of enlightenment is engendered in it from its very creation, but that if this state is left to continue without effort toward improvement, then it will become like a tree left uncultivated or a tract of land for which no one cares. Even though it will not cease to produce ideas and insights on many things, like the wild tree which continues to give fruit, still these ideas will not be comparable with those upon which effort has been expended. And just as the intellect requires education on the realities of existence, namely, those ideas whose content is its own exercise and without which its capacity will not emerge from potential to actuality, so also it needs education on intellect itself, so that its enlightenment will be complete and integral, without deficiency or confusion.

To this end the wise men of former times have toiled to arrange and classify the paths of the intellect, and to clarify its laws correctly, to discern the contingencies of intellect in the course of its operation, in both success and failure, in correct concepts and in falsehood, so as to elucidate the precautions necessary in inquiry for mistakes to be avoided, and to provide the assistance required for the correct conclusion. This study is called "logic"; and as I have seen the great need that is upon us in this matter, under which we would be unable to enter the portals of wisdom and to avail ourselves of its delights appropriately, I have chosen to arrange these brief extracts in such a manner as I saw fit for a comprehensive presentation. I have taken the majority of them from earlier works, in other languages, and rendered them into Hebrew for the benefit of our people, and I have also added further concepts, developed and adapted from what I found before me, in such a way as I thought most suitable; and so now, dear reader, arise and inquire, understand and grow in sweetness and knowledge, such as will gratify your soul.

APPENDIX 1
HISTORICAL BACKGROUND

PADUA AND THE ITALIAN GHETTO

Padua is situated about thirty miles inland from Venice, near the river Brenta, on the fertile and low-lying plain surrounding the river Po, the great river of northern Italy, which waters all the land between the Alps and the Apennines and contains the large cities of Turin and Milan. This area has since early times been one of the most active and prosperous settlements in all the world: rich in crops of every kind, including rice, and originally the source of gold and precious stones, it supported a civilized way of life before the Romans, and it has survived every change in history to continue in importance up to the present day. Padua has been a part of this story for almost its entire history, but its best years came during the Renaissance period when, as part of the giant Venetian economy, it became a manufacturing town for fine textiles brought from India and the Far East and developed its university to world prominence in the arts and sciences.

The Jewish community had existed before the Venetians took over, but in the years that followed, it grew rapidly by immigration from many lands, especially after the expulsion from Spain. Its situation was very favorable, and even the imposition of residential segregation in 1516, the first instance in Europe, was slow to affect conditions. The ghetto of Padua was not closed until 1601, by which time all Jews were required to wear the distinguishing badge and placed under restrictions in trade and the professions, but the ghettos had already become strong centers of Hebrew printing, and this enabled the Jews to carry on their spiritual life without difficulty. This coincidence of the rise of the ghetto with the end of manuscript learning has led to suggestions that the restrictions were only imposed because the innovation of printing had given added strength to the Jews and enabled them to spread their ideas.

The Paduan ghetto was grouped around a small square where the synagogues stood: they were known by the Italian name of *scuola* or "*shul*." There was an Ashkenazi building that served as *bet midrash* for the whole town, a Sephardi synagogue built in 1617 on the initiative of the influential Marini family, and a synagogue of the Roman or Italyeni rite, which is the only one remaining today. The *aron kodesh* of the Sephardi synagogue was dedicated in the presence of the Ramchal and bears the names of several of his closest associates;

it is now in the Hechal Shlomo synagogue in Jerusalem, the most notable relic in existence today associated with his person.

The ghetto was always known to the Jews
themselves as the "*Hatzer*," or courtyard. It had
five gates, each one bearing an inscription in Hebrew and Latin forbidding both Jews and Christians to approach the gates at night. The central
piazza ("square") was used for markets, and a special open-air market was held annually on Purim.
The buildings were constructed very tall because
of the space restrictions imposed on the community, making the ghetto visible from far away and
leading to great anxiety about the risks of fire and
disease. Plague visited the ghetto on several occasions, and half the population died from it in
1630–1631. Until 1715, the Jews were periodically
compelled to listen to conversionist sermons in
the churches. In 1684, the population sacked the
ghetto after rumors that the Jews had helped the
Turks against Venice in the siege of Budapest, and
loss of life was only narrowly averted by the inter-
vention of the army. In the tradition of the times
a special "local Purim," known as "*Purim-di-Buda*,"
was instituted for the anniversary of the deliverance.

In the mid-seventeenth century, the Venetians
suppressed the Jewish loan banks, and by the time
of the Ramchal, the Jews were engaged mainly in
commerce, mostly in textiles and jewelry. The
aristocrats of the community were the Spanish
and Portuguese, wholesalers and importers of fine
cloth. Below them was a secure middle class of
smaller traders and artisans in textiles; at the bot-

tom was the large, poorer class of street traders and ragpickers, who went about the districts buying old clothes to renovate or cut up for secondhand cloth, and whose voices in the streets were so characteristic of the ghetto and its times. Numerous health problems existed among them because of the unclean nature of the work and the restrictive economic circumstances.

Houses in the ghetto were owned by Christians, and the Jews acquired from them a fixed tenancy, which could be inherited or sold. This concept gained acceptance in Jewish law from the concept of "*hazakah*," and by a combination of Latin and Italianized Hebrew, the tenancy was known in Italian as the *jus gazaga*. The language was Judeo-Italian, a form of the main language, like Yiddish or Ladino, with Hebrew constructions and expressions, such as *dabberare*, ("to speak"), and a Jew could always be distinguished by his way of speaking. The ghetto had a reputation for noisiness, possibly because of the overcrowding, and a certain high-pitched tone of voice became proverbial; the slang term among the Italians for a noisy crowd was "a ghetto." Food was plentiful in the rich agricultural area, and certain vegetables such as eggplant, artichokes, and fennel were eaten only by Jews. Dishes made from them became famous, and the *Shabbat* and festivals had a whole range of delightful foods distinctive to the locality.

The statutory Jewish dress was a special hat, covered with crimson cloth and edged with black. Its use was rigorously enforced, and, as in other instances, the Jews tended to regard it as an emblem of their "citizenship of the Torah," and thus

a mark of honor. The ghetto abounded in benevolent organizations and fraternities; each trade and
profession had its own guild and saw to the wel-
fare of its members. There was a lodging house for
poor strangers, and a regular inn for prosperous
travelers as well.

The community itself was organized for its
autonomous self-government as *Universita degli
Ebrei* ("Congregation of the Hebrews"), but not
everyone theoretically eligible was in fact a contributing member of this; politics and external relationships were regarded as the province of the
elite few. Thus, it was difficult to raise taxes for general purposes, and in Padua special collection
boxes were set up in the public square at particular times for people to give contributions. This
method met with only limited success, and the
communal chest was often close to bankruptcy.
Frequent special tax demands by the government
on the *Universita* added to a feeling of burden and
harassment. With all this, though, the ghetto was
still a place rich in kindness and continuity: the
high standards of Torah learning throughout the
social strata surrounding the great scholars created
an atmosphere of respect and celebration.

AMSTERDAM

The Jewish community of Amsterdam is one that
occupies a unique place in history. There were
Jews in the Netherlands under the dukes of the
Middle Ages, but they were expelled after the Black
Death agitations, leaving no presence behind when

Spanish rule took over in the sixteenth century. The Netherlands became mainly Protestant at that time, and a climate of opposition to Spanish Catholic rule found its focus around the small Republic of the United Provinces, which had remained free with Amsterdam as its capital. There followed a war of independence. and a Dutch republic was established, a natural haven for Sephardi Jews fleeing the Marrano oppressions in Portugal and Spain.

In the extremity of the country's struggle for independence, the Dutch soon recognized the need of the Jews to found a safe haven from absolutist rule, and they began to show interest in Torah as a value system, asking what it really was and what advice it might contain for their betterment and consolidation. The non-Jewish intelligentsia were soon associating with learned Jews as colleagues and friends, in a completely different way from the rejectionist, book-burning reaction of the Church-dominated Middle Ages. The Noachide Laws were discussed; the scientific and philosophical issues of the time were aired; the paintings of Rembrandt and his school give us a glimpse of a society where destiny was examined in religious terms to the highest level of understanding.

The Dutch were the proprietors of the world's most dynamic and expansive empire of seaborne commerce, applying to the entire overseas world the techniques of the earlier Venetian Republic within the Mediterranean. They pioneered the joint-stock company and abolished the Church prohibition on interest-bearing loans that had caused so much distress to Jews, thus creating an economy in which Jews and non-Jews worked and invested together for the first time. The trades of jewelry processing, silk weaving, and sugar refining were largely in Jewish hands. Optical goods were manufactured for export in great quantities; the telescope was a Dutch invention, which had proved very useful in the war against the Spaniards. The Ramchal was directed to this trade for his personal income on arrival. It was also possible to found another great center of Hebrew printing, and this served to consolidate the spiritual life of the community, with very high standards in production, which placed the output in demand in other countries as well.

In the early days there was turbulence among intellectuals within the community over the Shabbatean movement and an early version of assimilationist pressure from the surrounding culture, which later came to be felt so strongly. There were writers and philosophers, often engaged in the medical profession, who became headstrong and disinclined to accept contradiction, and they were locked in conflict with a capable Rabbinate influenced by the Kabbalah of the Ari-zal. This public turmoil was already on the wane by the time of the Ramchal's arrival, and his presence helped to settle the atmosphere in the community still further.

The Jews could afford to construct their buildings in keeping with their social and economic status, and one of the inheritances we have from this early time is the great Spanish and Portuguese synagogue in the Jewish quarter. This structure became the model for all future synagogues in the West, and its architectural character expresses the wide horizons and sense of fulfillment its community had. Left intact by the Nazis, it stands today as a testimony to the spirit of Jewry in exile, a monument to a great advance toward the Redemption and to its members' fortitude and skill.

POLITICAL EVENTS
IN EIGHTEENTH-CENTURY EUROPE

The "wars of religion" in sixteenth- and seventeenth-century Europe, which followed on the collapse of the papal power with the coming of the Reformation, left France as the clear leader on the Continent and, by example, in the wider world. All hope of German unity had been destroyed by the fighting, and with England still much smaller in population and resources, everyone was aware that events in France held the key to the future. About a quarter of France had turned Protestant, and it seemed for a time that they might gain predominance under their gifted leader Henry of Navarre, but in a consummate act of treachery, he agreed to become a Catholic in order to obtain the throne; subsequently, he let the Catholics of Paris loose on their Protestant neighbors in a night of massacre that left him free from organized challenge.

Under Catholic rule, the Protestants of France were worn down, harried, and eventually expelled, and by these means the country achieved unity under a centralized monarchical regime. In the context of the Counter-Reformation, this meant the assertion of the principle of personal jurisdiction vested in kings, the assertion that their rule owed nothing to any principle outside themselves, and that no law or judge had jurisdiction over them.

This view was summed up most succinctly by King Louis XIV of France, who had surprised everyone from his own mother on down by running the government in person and making a huge success out of it, in his famous maxim: "The state is me." Many saw this as a manifestation of the tendency of kings to make themselves into objects of idolatrous worship, parallel to the Church claim that Jesus or his priests also could say that religion "is me."

In England, his ally Charles I had tried to impose this same doctrine on his own subjects by deliberately raising taxes unconstitutionally, and he was defeated in battle and executed for this offense against the rule of law. At this same juncture, the readmission of the Jews to England was successfully negotiated, casting the "Jewish vote" in favor of constitutional government by showing that the king's execution had been in accordance with law and not a mere dynastic supplanting or an illegal act of rebellion.

Louis brought industry and commerce under government control and created a powerful army that, under the command of several marshals of France whose military abilities he cultivated to the maximum level of expertise, he used in wars for continental hegemony. In 1672 he accompanied his troops into Holland in an attempt to subdue its freedoms, based as they were on the Jewish alliance, and this was the first emergence of the concept of "war against the Jews," as the world has come to know it up to the present time. Near the end of his reign, he attacked the Austrian Empire, seeking control of the strategic "Bohemian quadrilateral," which confers dominance of all of central Europe upon the occupier; but the coalition of nations opposed to him sent the small but highly trained English army into the balance against him at the critical moment in the campaign. Its commander, John Churchill, duke of Marlborough, defeated Louis' forces at the Battle of Blenheim in 1711. Thus, the French monarchy lost the initiative soon before Louis himself left the succession to his five-year-old great-grandson.

The French army had suffered a great loss in prestige, which was confirmed throughout the eighteenth century by failure in battle against the British in India and in North America. This lack of imperial success created a financial crisis in the country, exacerbated by the burdens of debt left by Louis' military expenditures. This, in turn, encouraged class antagonisms, and the large mass of career professional military officers who had been awarded the top rank in the state by Louis were soon turning against the monarchy as such, following revolutionary philosophies in the expectation that they would be the ones to put them into practice.

When violence erupted on the streets of Paris in 1789, the army soon let it be known that it would not fire to save the monarchy, and it was not long before the revolutionary generals took over the government itself. It was inevitable with the galaxy of military talent they possessed that they would soon try once more to make France into a conquering power; in the person of Napoleon, the "godless" successor to the "Catholic" ambitions of Louis, they found one of their number to undertake the task.

Thus, at the time of the Ramchal, Europe existed under a French hegemony that, though prosperous and united, did not have the qualities of endurance. It was strong in the manufacturing industry, the leader in this respect during the craft era before mechanization, and this high level of quality control, utilizing the personal integrity of the craftsman, set the tone for the society as a whole, even for Jews in their spiritual service in lands under its influence. The chasidic movement by contrast originated in the rural life of Eastern Europe, so economically underdeveloped that the aspect of pure simplicity within Torah wisdom became the most significant factor.

The turmoil of the Reformation and Counter-Reformation had also discredited religion in the public mind, and though there was a strong demand for public morality, a "worldliness" of outlook had come to prevail, particularly under Louis' economic renewal. France had very few Jewish subjects of its own to exercise an influence on conditions, and all through the Torah world, it came to be seen as the home of every tendency most opposed to Jewish teaching, a reputation confirmed during Napoleon's reign with his disestablishment of the rabbinic autonomy in the lands he conquered.

Because of the close control over Italy, which was and remains a cornerstone of French foreign

policy, the Jews there were more exposed than any
to the winds that were blowing. In the main they
were still sheltered by their autonomy in the ghetto,
but their ancient way of life there could not continue, and the Ramchal, like other great *tzaddikim*,
knew full well what to say and to do in his time,
to bring them out to their redemptive goal.

ERETZ YISRAEL UNDER THE TURKS

At the start of the sixteenth century, *Eretz Yisrael*
was ruled from Egypt by the Mamelukes, a strange
dynasty of warriors originating from freed slaves,
who did not pass on their dominion to their own
sons but adopted young boys and brought them
up in the disciplines of soldiering. Their power
became menaced from the north by the Ottoman
Turks, descendants of an assembly of central Asian
tribes who had conquered the Anatolian peninsula
from Byzantium for Islam; in 1516 the dynamic
Sultan Selim I captured *Eretz Yisrael* from them by
a ruse of war. The Turks pretended to be preparing
for a march on Persia, thus inducing the Mamelukes to advance toward Syria and leave their supply bases behind. His son Suleiman the Magnifi-
cent proved to be the real founder of the Turkish
Empire; he quelled a rebellion by the native-born
wali ("viceroy") of *Eretz Yisrael*, executed him, and
brought the country firmly under Turkish control
by placing Turks in all leading positions and con-
structing the extensive walls for Jerusalem that can
be seen today.

His influence in the system of government

lasted for centuries; he allocated land to a number of feudal deputies (*sanjak*), who were then responsible for raising taxes and military forces to support the central imperial ruler. Soon the country grew in security and prosperity, and the population increased as agriculture became productive again, doubling within fifty years of the conquest. Jews were engaged in producing wine and honey, and many were attracted to the Land by the favorable circumstances. At this time, Jews were flooding into the Turkish territories of the Near East and Balkans from Spain, and the rabbinic leaders secured the goodwill of the Turkish authorities on their arrival for the proposition that their community as a whole would be best consolidated by establishing Torah scholarship in *Eretz Yisrael*. Sephardi influence became dominant in the Land, and many outstanding scholars such as R. Yosef Caro, R. Yitzchak Luria, and R. Moshe Cordovero were able to settle in Safed and to make it a center of spiritual discovery and renewal for the entire Jewish world.

However, the situation deteriorated within a hundred years as the elite Turkish military force, the Janissaries, became steadily greedier and more rebellious, and border nations such as the Druse took advantage of the decline in discipline. Attempts to restore order from Constantinople met with failure, and banditry began to increase, leading to a rapid economic decline. The central government was inclined to form temporary alliances with anyone it felt could help it out of its immediate problems, and thus, the Jewish alliance was dispensed with. The former center in Safed became unsafe, as was shown by the decision of the *Shelah*, Rabbi Yeshaya Horowitz, to settle in Jerusalem in 1621. The city of Gaza rose in importance because of its closeness to Egypt, and it was there that Shabetai Zvi went when he came to the country. His movement of desperation caused the Turks concern over their entire rulership and further lowered the Jews in their estimation after he was induced to convert to Islam.

By the start of the eighteenth century, the Ottoman Empire had been forced to sign several humiliating treaties with the European powers, especially with Russia, which gained an intercessionary right on behalf of the Christian subjects of the sultan and over the "holy places" in the Land. Drug abuse and other failings gained a hold on the Turkish leadership, and with the evident weakness of the central power, it became necessary for local rulers to raise private armies from among the tribesmen, to be used for any governmental or personal purpose they chose. These armies became the main source of the anarchy that followed; wars of a "gangster" variety spread among the Pashas, who formed their own alliances with foreign powers and seized the dwindling economic prizes there for the taking. These were the conditions surrounding the Ramchal during his years in the country. The Jewish community became much poorer, divided by the aftermath of the Shabbatean movement and isolated by the breakdown of communications. However, great efforts were made by world Jewry to maintain Jerusalem as a center, and it was the home of many great scholars, such as R. Shalom Sharabi, R. Chaim ben-Attar, and R. Gershon of Kitov, the Baal Shem Tov's brother-in-law.

Thus, at this time the country had entered an "unhistorical" phase of development, desolate and irrelevant to world affairs, without the consolidated society of the other states and Jewries of the time. Its true spiritual purposes were carried on privately, without widespread interest, and it was well understood that it had reached a level from which only worldwide philosophical changes could save it. Jews regarded it as dangerous to settle there, and they relied almost entirely on the concept of "*Eretz Yisrael* in exile," which their rabbinic autonomy gave them in the lands of dispersion. When Napoleon withdrew this internal citizenship, which had recognized Jews legally as a people originating from *Eretz Yisrael* itself, the national identity reverted to the point of origin. Jews who had been left with no other form of identification thus began to proclaim that *Eretz Yisrael* was rightfully theirs, and though this reversion at first took a secular form due to the disruption in educational conditions, its path had already been paved by the Ramchal and the other *tzaddikim* who had returned under the previous adverse circumstances.

THE LUZZATTO FAMILY

No direct descendants of the Ramchal are now living, but the Luzzatto family (sometimes also spelled Luzzatti) is extensive and distinguished in Italy and all over the world. It originated from the village of Lausitz in Bavaria, and after becoming

established in Venice, spread out to Padua and
other nearby Jewish centers as they came under
Venetian rule. The halachic author Jacob ben Isaac
Luzzatto of sixteenth-century Safed also traces his
ancestry to the family.

In 1595 two brothers from Venice, Abraham
and Benedetto Luzzatto, settled in the small up-
land town of San Daniele di Friuli, founding a
third main branch of the family. Benedetto's two
sons Ephraim and Isaac, both doctors, also wrote
poetry, and a later descendant Mordechai (Marco)
was an author and translator of halachic works.
The Venetian government decided in 1777 to move
the Jews out of the smaller settlements and gather
them in the capital; in consequence of this, one
relative from San Daniele di Friuli decided to go
instead to Trieste. This was Hezekiah, who became
the father of Shmuel David Luzzatto, the first "en-
lightened" member of the family, a historian and
author on Jewish topics and the ancestor of the
family branch best known for secular distinction.
Another relative, Luigi Luzzatti, became in 1910
the first professing Jewish prime minister of Italy
or any other European country.

APPENDIX 2

THE WORKS OF RAMCHAL

The most important printed source for the life of the Ramchal is the Hebrew *sefer Yarim Moshe,* with its collection of letters and other documents pertaining to the events described. There is a large body of material extant in manuscript, mostly in the library of the Jewish Theological Seminary in New York, which has the complete collection of documents concerning the Venetian persecution, but examples also exist in the Jewish National and University Library in Yerushalayim, and a few remain in private hands.

Most of the Ramchal's works were not published in his lifetime but circulated in manuscript or small, privately printed editions. Many that were subsequently published are again out of print, including the complete poems, which came out in Tel Aviv in the 1920s. Manuscript material that remained unpublished has recently been gathered

171

together and issued in Israel under various titles,
including the *Ginzei Ramchal*, but some items are
still uncompiled. The following list of publication
dates refers to the first full printed edition intended for general readership, and the titles mentioned are those of more general interest only.

Shir Zahav Lichvod Concili	Venice, 1723
Lashon Limudim	Mantua, 1727
Shir Chanukat ha-Aron	Venice, 1729
Shir al-Mos R. Binyamin	
Cohen Vitali	Venice, 1730
Mesillat Yesharim	Amsterdam, 1740
Derech Tevunot	Amsterdam, 1742
Layesharim Tehillah	Amsterdam, 1743
Derech Chochmah	
Maamar ha-Chochmah	
Maamar ha-Aggadot	Amsterdam, 1783
Maamar ha-Ikkarim	
Hoker u-Mekubbal	Sklov, 1784
Kalach Pit'chei Chochmah	Koretz, 1785
Migdal Oz	Leipzig, 1837
Daat Tevunot	Warsaw, 1889
Klalei Chochmat ha-Emet	Warsaw, 1889
Derech Hashem	Amsterdam, 1896
Maasei Shimshon	Tel Aviv, 1927

APPENDIX 3

CHRONOLOGY

1698 Birth of R. Yisrael Baal Shem Tov.

1701 First new synagogue built in England after the Readmission.

1707 Birth of R. Moshe Chaim Luzzatto, Ramchal.

1712 Russia's reforming czar, Peter the Great, founds city of St. Petersburg on Baltic coast captured from Sweden.

Book *Curiosa Americana* by Cotton Mather, the first book about America by an American, published in Boston.

1714 British Crown passes to George I, Elector of Hanover.

Book *Reasons for Naturalizing the Jews* by John Toland published in London.

1715 Death of Louis XIV; French Crown passes to his great-grandson, then five years old, and the royal power is given to the duke of Orleans as regent.

Armed rising in Scotland against the Hanoverian king.

1716 Emperor of China bans Christianity, thus closing the country to the outside world.

1717 Turkish practice of inoculation against small-pox introduced into Europe.

1718 Founding of New Orleans at the mouth of the Mississippi, named after the regent of France.

1719 Rabbi Jonathan Eybeshutz in Prague obtains license to print the whole Talmud for the first time since the banning edicts of the Middle Ages.

1720 London Stock Exchange crashes after speculation in overseas investments, nicknamed "South Sea Bubble."

Spanish occupation of Texas.

Birth of Rabbi Eliyahu Kramer, Gaon of Vilna.

1721 First regular mail service between England and America.

1725 Death of Czar Peter the Great.

1727 First treaty between emperors of Russia and China delineating their border in central Asia.

Death of Sir Isaac Newton.

First planting of coffee in Brazil.

Ramchal receives mysterious *maggid* and organizes Holy Society in Padua.

1729 Benjamin Franklin and his brother James open *Pennsylvania Gazette* newspaper in Philadelphia.

Letter concerning *maggid* reaches Rabbi Moshe Chagis, opponent of Ramchal.

1730 **Ramchal agrees to discontinue activities of Holy Society.**

1731 **Marriage of Ramchal.**

1732 Birth of George Washington.

1734 Emergence of Baal Shem Tov to leadership.

Ramchal leaves Padua for Amsterdam under pressure from R. Moshe Chagis.

1735 *Systema Naturae* by Linnaeus (Carl von Linne) published in Leyden.

1737 Ghetto of Vilna burned down in rioting and rebuilt with help from the community of Amsterdam.

1740 Death of Emperor Charles VI of Austria, leading to War of Austrian Succession between Britain and France over large claims in Italy and Germany. Crown passes to his daughter Maria Theresa.

Crown of Prussia, the state around which all the German lands became unified passes to Frederick the Great, who promotes education and awards freedoms of speech and the press but also begins buildup of the German army.

Act of the British Parliament awards right of naturalization to Jews resident in the American colonies, but a subsequent attempt to extend the same law to Britain itself leads to fall of the government after a nationwide agitation.

Ramchal publishes *The Path of the Just* in Amsterdam.

1742 Rabbi Chaim ben-Attar, Or ha-Chaim, and his followers arrive in Jerusalem.

1743 Birth of Thomas Jefferson.

Ramchal arrives in *Eretz Yisrael*.

1744 British and French armies, composed of native troops with European officers, fight in India for control of the south of the country.

Expulsion of the Jews from Prague by Empress Maria Theresa of Austria, to be readmitted four years later.

1745 Second rising in Scotland against the Hanoverian dynasty; a rebel army invades England but is pursued back into Scotland and defeated in the last pitched battle on the British mainland.

Birth of Rabbi Schneur Zalman of Liadi.

1746 Passing of Ramchal and burial in Tiberias.

1747 Baal Shem Tov holds colloquy with *Mashiach* on the manner of the redemption.

1750 Frederick the Great of Prussia grants *Toleranzpatent*, semiliberal law granting limited freedoms and opening some professions to Jews, but still under general restriction.

CREDITS

The author gratefully acknowledges permission to quote from the following sources:

The Way of God, by Moshe Chaim Luzzatto, trans. R. Shraga Silberstein and R. Aryeh Kaplan. Copyright © 1977 by Aryeh Kaplan. Published by Feldheim Publishers Ltd. Used by permission.

The Knowing Heart, by Moshe Chaim Luzzatto, trans. R. Shraga Silberstein. Copyright © 1982 by Feldheim Publishers. Published by Feldheim Publishers Ltd. Used by permission.

The Path of the Just, by Moshe Chaim Luzzatto, trans. R. Shraga Silberstein. Copyright © 1966 by Boys Town Jerusalem-Yaakov Feldheim. Published by Feldheim Publishers Ltd. Used by permission.

The Ways of Reason, by Moshe Chaim Luzzatto, trans. Rabbi David Sackton and Rabbi Chaim Tscholkowsky. Copyright © 1989 by Rabbi David Sackton and Rabbi Chaim Tscholkowsky. Published by Feldheim Publishers Ltd. Used by permission.

INDEX

Rabbi Yirmeyahu Bindman was born in Coventry, England, and received a degree in physics from London University in 1971. He is the author of *Lord George Gordon*, a dramatized biography of the eighteenth-century English convert to Judaism, and *The Seven Colors of the Rainbow*, an exposition of the Noachide Laws. He moved to Israel in 1979 and now lives in Jerusalem with his wife and children.